BATMAN™

THE ULTIMATE EVIL

B**A**T THE ULTIMATE

MAN™

EVIL

ANDREW VACHSS

ASPECT®

WARNER BOOKS

A Time Warner Company

Warner Books, Inc., 1271 Avenue of the Americas, New York, NY 10020

 A Time Warner Company

Printed in the United States of America
First printing: November 1995
10 9 8 7 6 5 4 3 2 1

Library of Congress Cataloging-in-Publication Data
Vachss, Andrew H.
    Batman : the ultimate evil / Andrew Vachss.
      p.   cm.
    ISBN 0-446-51912-X (hardcover)
    I. Title.
  PS3572.A33B38   1995
  813'.54—dc20   95-2281
                                            CIP

acknowledgments

David Joe Wirth
Geopolitics

James Eden Colbert
Warfare

Steven Korté
Foundation

this is for
all the
Children of the Secret

BATMAN™

THE ULTIMATE EVIL

If Paris is the City of Light, what then is Gotham?

From its downtown Government Center where buildings crowd each other like subway passengers, to its midtown glitz of luxury hotels and four-star restaurants casually dispersed among ultra-ultra shops, to the uptown splendor of its high-rise co-ops and condos, Gotham stands as an international symbol of cosmopolitan success.

Airline pilots love to bank low over the city before landing at Gotham Airport, treating the passengers avidly lining the windows to the magnificent skyline. Viewed from above, Gotham by night resembles nothing so much as a ribbon of diamonds artfully arranged on a pad of deep, rich black velvet.

But closer to ground zero, the view changes. The black velvet has an illumination all its own—the cold garish neon of the sex industry, the feverish light in the dead eyes of desperate drug addicts, the inadequate streetlights creating pools of shadow in which muggers patiently wait.

Deeper down in the crosstown depths of the city, the only light is artificial . . . as man-made as evil itself.

And the only language spoken is the unspeakable.

The mid-rise apartment complex stood proudly just inside the ribbon of light, two blocks over from the crosstown darkness. The two-block safety cushion was called Bordertown by the good citizens who walked through it on their way to work every day. But the cops who patrolled it at night called it by another name—the DMZ.

The developer of the complex had received a massive tax break from the City Council in exchange for his pledge to create a highly prized area of "urban green." Three of the apartment buildings were constructed at a slight angle to the street so that their intersection formed a triangle. The developer emphasized the triangle theme with a concrete walkway surrounding a patch of grass. The walkway was dotted with wrought iron benches.

"Don't tell me about the Ginza, don't tell me about

Hong Kong," the developer had bragged at a black-tie party for one of his wife's pet charities. "Maybe there are cities where they rent for a few bucks more per square foot, but when it comes to the bottom line, Gotham is king of the heap. For what I got for building those dinky little plazas the City Council loves so much, you'd have to cover the ground with uranium to make it worth any more."

"What do people use the plazas for?" a vapid young woman asked.

"Damned if I know," the developer said.

The developer's words joined the whisper-stream that flowed throughout the city, blending with other voices, other words . . .

In the plaza, a man looked up, but not at the sky. Lying on his back on one of the decorative wrought iron benches with only a padding of discarded newspapers as a mattress, the homeless man watched the geometric pattern made by the random lighting of windows in the apartment complex. His eyes filmed with sadness as he recalled the time when he too lived among the strivers, a proud member of the middle class, upwardly mobile, aspiring to wealth, driven by an insatiable ambition to acquire . . . what?

"Things," the homeless man thought to himself, "just things. Inanimate, temporary *things*." They had never lasted long—neither did the pleasure each new acquisition had so alluringly promised.

The whisper-streams flowed unimpeded throughout Gotham, vacuuming bits and pieces into their depths, cascading into a dark river of rumor, innuendo, mystery, and myth.

If the homeless man's gaze had taken a slightly higher

arc, if his distance vision had been sufficiently sharp, he might have locked eyes with a creature of the night, a shadow-shrouded figure watching from a perch atop the mid-rise building.

He might have seen the Batman.

Or, more correctly, he might have seen a gray-and-black-clad figure, a caped and cowled masterpiece of urban camouflage. He might have seen a . . . presence. Despite the thousands of criminals the Batman had faced in his years of subterranean combat, not a single one could claim to have seen the man behind the mask. The Batman was a hyperhuman phenomenon, a living ghost—skillfully surfing the whisper-stream throughout Gotham's underworld, a terror to terrorists.

Some said the Batman was a rumor himself. Just an exaggerated legend . . . like the alligators in the sewers.

But nobody said it loud. And nobody said it long.

The Batman stood motionless, his combat-trained eyes sweeping the ground, focusing and refocusing as rapidly and smoothly as a falcon's.

"*How* you see is stronger than *what* you see," the crime fighter thought, recalling one of his earliest martial arts lessons. The whisper-stream swirled into the triangular park, a temporary delta in an infinite river. The Batman had followed the stream patiently. Now he willed himself into a rest-state, slowing his heart and lungs, going quietly inside himself, no longer using just his eyes but his whole body as a sensor.

They would come soon. The Batman knew this. And for all his scientific knowledge, for all his sophisticated machinery, he could not have said precisely *how* he knew.

The homeless man took out a crumpled cigarette, his last one. He scratched behind his ear, ruefully remembering how he used to enjoy a rich Cuban cigar every night with a glass of claret before he retired to his bedroom. "At least I'm free now," he thought, patting his pockets, the cigarette dangling from his lips.

"Looking for a match, old man?"

The homeless man sat up suddenly, seeing the three teenagers standing a few feet away, their leather-jacketed bodies forming a triangle as though to mock the plaza itself. The homeless man was paralyzed with fear. He didn't read the newspapers, but he listened to the whisper-stream. And he knew what the gang wanted.

"Leave me alone!" he shouted. But the shout came out a whine, low-pitched and weak—a goad to the gang. The leader, the one who spoke first, snapped his fingers. A flame shot out, almost a foot high.

The flame made another of the boys giggle—a high-pitched cackle as jagged as broken glass. The third youth pulled a plastic squeeze bottle from inside his jacket. The homeless man knew what was inside that bottle . . . he would have known even if the sharp smell of gasoline hadn't filled the plaza.

"Bum Burning" they called it—the latest sadistic entertainment for the random-violence youth gangs that stalked parts of Gotham. It was easy enough—you find a homeless person sleeping, you douse him with gasoline . . . then you toss on a flaming match and watch the fun.

"I'm not a bum!" the homeless man screamed in his mind. "I'm a person! I have a name!"

But no sound came out.

The gang started its dance, moving into practiced positions, guarding against the victim trying to make a run for it. The homeless man felt the will to resist run out of him like sand through open fingers.

"Douse him, Raj!" the giggler said.

The homeless man covered his face. The gang closed in, the giggler forcing the homeless man's shoulders back against the bench. The homeless man opened his eyes, staring into the face of his tormentor, desperately seeking . . . what? Understanding, human compassion? . . . but all the homeless man saw was the self-absorbed gaze of a psychopath whose idea of fun was tormenting others. The homeless man sucked in one last breath to try and scream when . . .

. . . a piece of the night dropped from the sky, landing softly on the ground.

The Batman—Stalker of Predators.

"It's all over," he said, snapping his flowing cape out with both fists to block all escape, converting it from parachute to shield in the same motion. The opaque eye slots in his cowl burned with a cold fire.

"Get him, Raj!" the leader yelled, falling into a knife fighter's crouch, the small blowtorch extended in front of him. The teenager with the plastic squeeze bottle leaped forward, shooting a fine mist of gasoline at the Batman. The crime fighter stood his ground, not moving even when the leader triggered his blowtorch. A tongue of flame leaped the gap to the gasoline-soaked masked man.

The Batman went up in flames!

But two rapid flaps of his cape extinguished the blaze as quickly as it had begun.

And the Batman stood as he had stood before, as inexorable as death itself.

The homeless man watched in amazement as the gang leader dropped his blowtorch and raised his hands. The one they had called Raj tossed away his squeeze bottle and followed suit.

But the giggler pulled a gun. The chrome semiautomatic pistol gleamed in his hand. Another psychotic giggle escaped his lips as he leveled the weapon at the still-standing Batman. "Let's see you laugh *this* one off!" he shouted.

As the giggler squeezed the trigger, the Batman flicked his left hand. His black cape moved in that direction, but his body was already in motion to the right. The Batman hit the ground in a modified forward roll. A piston-powered boot slammed into the giggler's chest, knocking him backward. The gun discharged into the air.

The Batman rolled smoothly to his feet, looking down at the giggler. The young man was holding his rib cage and whimpering.

After that, it only took a quick call on the Batman's direct-link transmitter to bring a pair of squad cars to the plaza. As the police pulled up, the Batman vanished into the night, leaving only a profoundly moved homeless man to explain the three handcuffed terrorists.

It was not enough.

Maybe it would *never* be enough.

Even as the Batmobile headed for home under cover of darkness, sliding smoothly through a series of switchbacks on a rarely used country road, the masked man at the wheel was bombarded with intrusive thoughts. Always the same theme—in the war between criminals and crusaders, only the criminals found a perpetually renewable source of troops. As the crusaders aged, they faced wave after wave of fresh combatants.

It was like swimming toward the horizon, the Batman thought bitterly.

But if you stop swimming . . . you drown.

The rows of tiny LED sensors flashed off and on, reporting on everything from the condition of the road ahead to any activity around the hidden entrance to the Batcave. All clear.

The Batmobile stopped just inside the camouflaged entrance so that the security cameras could record visual data. In the next of the chambered air locks, a robot arm smoothly extended. As it moved slowly toward the Batmobile, a slot opened just behind the Batmobile's left front wheel. The robot arm extruded a flat disc about the size of two credit cards. The vehicle's slot accepted the disc. Inside the Batmobile, the computer screen read:

Analyzing Data Input. Please wait . . .

The Batman sat quietly until the robot arm withdrew the disc. He heard the faint coupling sound as a massive hydraulic lift raised the Batmobile off the ground. No more driving was required—the machinery would do the rest. And if any vehicle other than the Batmobile tried to enter the inner chambers without achieving computer clearance, the hydraulic lift would perform quite another function.

Deep inside, there was a faint hiss as the canopy retracted so that the Batman could climb out. The crime fighter started for the elevator that would carry him up and out—out of the Batcave and into another life. Suddenly he stopped and went over to the console of a giant mainframe computer. He sat before the screen and started using the keyboard to ask questions.

"Are you all right, Master Bruce?" The speaker was a tall, dignified man dressed in an immaculate black suit. He was gently shaking the shoulder of the Batman, a look of deep concern on his patrician face.

The Batman snapped awake. "I'm fine, Alfred," he said. "I was just doing some data analysis—I must have fallen asleep."

"You came in almost three hours ago," Alfred said. "I marked the time when the indicator lights flashed upstairs. I wasn't worried at first—the computer that monitors your vital signs whenever you return showed no problems. But when I didn't hear from . . ."

"It's okay, my old friend," the Batman said. "I guess I must have gotten lost in my thoughts, that's all."

"The same thoughts?" Alfred asked.

"Yes," the Batman said, tilting back his cowl as he spoke. "But I'm fine. A couple of hours' sleep, a quick shower and shave, and I'll be right on time for the museum opening."

"Whatever you say, sir," Alfred replied, obviously dissatisfied with the response.

The Batman opened his mouth as though to explain, but snapped it shut as Alfred turned his back and exited the cave.

The Gotham Museum was celebrating a new wing by holding an exclusive viewing before it was opened to the public. Attendance was by invitation only. *Engraved* invitation—the Board of Directors was sparing no expense, having long since realized that while museums may be intended for the public, it is always private capital that keeps them open.

Bruce Wayne watched as the uniformed guard demanded proof before letting a young couple pass inside. The guard's voice was haughty and hostile all at the same time. Bruce Wayne reached for the inside pocket of his midnight-blue tuxedo, pleased but not surprised to discover that Alfred had remembered to include the invitation. But his attempt to show it to the uniformed guard was waved away with a respectful bow. "Everybody knows who *you* are, Mr. Wayne," the guard said, a servile whine to his voice that grated on the billionaire's already-raw nerves. He glanced at the guard's chest, noting a brass nameplate. "Thank you, Otto," he said, walking past the purple velvet ropes into the new wing of the museum.

The new wing was to be called *Now and Today*. It would concentrate on current topics of social and cultural importance. The first exhibit, "The Greatness of Gotham," was already in place, showing the city's progress, from a fur-trading outpost to a riverfront town more noted for its gambling casinos than for its civic achievements, to the thriving megalopolis it was today.

Bruce Wayne, billionaire, was always welcome at such events. Indeed, to do otherwise than invite him would be to ignore the single largest source of charitable contributions in all of Gotham. "Wayne" might be at the end of any alphabetized list, but it was the first name any fundraiser tried.

Of the four million dollars raised for the new museum wing, Bruce Wayne had personally written a check for five hundred thousand. He strolled aimlessly through the exhibit, shaking hands as many times as a politician, his face a mask of politeness. Gotham had many faces, many facets, but the Gotham so proudly displayed in the new exhibit was a triumph of public relations—it validated the belief that reality is what people are allowed to see, not what actually exists. As far as the "Greatness of Gotham" exhibit was concerned, the magnificent city was untouched by crime, homelessness, poverty, disease . . . or any of the other ills that so characterized urban life in the nineties. As Bruce Wayne traversed the exhibit, he felt he was walking a tightrope along that river of diamonds Gotham became when viewed from on high at night. In the museum exhibit, the fringe areas had all been sanitized. Or eliminated entirely.

"Bruce! Oh, Bruce! Over here!"

He looked toward the source of the genteel shouting and spotted the infamous Diana Dorchester, a woman who fancied herself royalty because her husband's money generated a constant flow of sycophants trailing in her wake. Although a relatively young woman, her total self-absorption gave her an edge even on the elderly dowagers who had spent decades solidifying their precious social positions.

Bruce Wayne slowly made his way over to Dame Diana (as she was called in the gossip columns), dreading the encounter but seeing it as unavoidable. "Oh, Bruce," she trilled, "isn't it just beautiful what they've done with the space?"

"Beautiful," he agreed, already looking around for an exit.

"It is so important to really make a difference," Diana proclaimed in a royal tone. She accepted the affirmative nods and murmurs of those around her as her due, basking in the approval of her inferiors.

But Bruce was mentally chewing on her words, wondering, for what seemed like the thousandth time in the past months, if the Batman was really, truly "making a difference." Years and years of frontline battles, and what did the good people of Gotham have to show for it? As quickly as law enforcement filled the prisons, new felons rose up to take the place of the incarcerated. Wasn't there a way . . . ?

"You call this PR stunt 'making a difference'?" A sarcastic female voice lanced through the small throng, its barbs aimed directly at Diana Dorchester. The speaker was a young woman, striding forward with determination, her white-blonde hair flowing behind her, her orange

eyes flashing. "An albino woman," Bruce Wayne thought.
"And a proud one too," noting the generously propor-
tioned body wrapped in a plain black jersey dress.

"I don't know your name, dear," Diana countered, "but
I recognize the rhetoric all too well. Each of us must decide
for ourselves how we make our civic contribution. The problem is, *you* want to make that decision for all of *us*. If you want
to feed the homeless or build playgrounds . . . or what*ever*,
you just run along and do it. For myself, I consider the stim-
ulation of civic pride to be a worthy endeavor!"

"Hear, hear!" several of Diana's entourage chanted.
Others voiced their approval and support, all eyes turned
to the albino woman.

"This exhibit has nothing to do with civic pride," she
said. "The Gotham it shows is *your* Gotham—it has nothing
to do with the way people actually live. But even the idle
rich aren't immune from crime. And you can't make *that*
go away with some phony exhibit."

"Oh *really*!" Diana hissed. "Actually, my dear, everybody
knows where crime comes from . . . from poverty, of course.
Anything that improves the image of Gotham attracts investors. And investors mean jobs. Certainly you can—"

"Poverty doesn't cause crime," the albino woman
interrupted. "People cause crime. Poverty doesn't cause
rape. It doesn't cause most murder either. We have to
take the—"

"Oh go find a soapbox," Diana said, dismissing the
other woman and turning to her entourage. "Shall we
move on? There is *so* much we haven't seen yet."

Bruce Wayne watched the group move away, grateful
for a moment of peace. But it wasn't to be. The albino
woman closed in on him, cheeks slightly flushed with

anger. "How come you didn't move along with the rest of them?" she demanded in a ready-for-combat voice.

"I've seen the exhibits," he replied mildly.

"Do you believe what she said . . . that poverty is what causes crime?"

"It's a contributor," Bruce replied. "But no rational person believes it's the sole cause. Where do *you* believe it comes from?"

"Like I said, it comes from—"

"People, I know," Bruce said. "But don't you feel that's a bit simplistic? The real question is *which* people, isn't it?"

Surprisingly, the exotic-looking woman flashed a dazzling smile. "Yes!" she said. "That *is* the question. And even though we know the answer, we don't do anything about it."

"And the answer is . . . ?"

"Children," the woman said. "I don't mean that children commit most of the crime—although they certainly commit an increasing amount of it—I mean that the maltreatment of children is the greatest single contributor to later criminal behavior."

"You mean like . . . child abuse? That sort of thing?"

"Yes, Mr. Wayne, I mean *exactly* 'that sort of thing,'" she answered. "In fact, that's what I do."

"I don't understand," Bruce said. "You apparently know my name, but I don't . . ."

"My name is Debra," she said. "Debra Kane. I'm a caseworker with the Gotham Child Protective Services."

"How did you—?"

"Get in? It was easy enough. My old college roommate was invited. She told me about it—she wasn't going anyway—so I borrowed her invitation."

"No," he said. "I don't mean that. How did you get into your . . . field, I guess."

"Believe it or not, it was a course I took in college," the woman said. "I wanted to be in the Peace Corps, but one of my professors showed us that children right here in Gotham . . . some of them anyway . . . are just as oppressed and mistreated as in any Third World country."

"He sounds like a man of compassion," Bruce Wayne said, an inquiring look on his face.

"*She* is," the woman replied. "Or, at least, she was. She was killed last year."

"Killed? How?"

"A gunshot, that's all we know. It's so sad . . . she was walking home after classes when she found herself in the middle of a gunfight between two gangs. Gangs of kids. She was accidentally hit, an innocent bystander. I wonder if those kids know who they killed. I wonder if they care . . ."

"I'd like to learn more . . . about children and crime, that is," Bruce Wayne said. "Could I call you sometime?"

"I'll save you the trouble," the exotic woman said. "If this is some kind of—"

"It's no come-on," he assured her.

The woman regarded the tall, handsome man standing before her, a man who spent more on the suit he was wearing than she earned in a month. But all her innate prejudice against the idle rich vanished when she looked into his eyes. She had seen that look before—a look of deep, elemental pain. Without another word, she wrote a telephone number on the back of her engraved invitation and handed it to Bruce. The Batman's alter ego bowed gravely, as to a martial arts instructor. The albino woman returned his bow. Then she turned her back and walked away.

Later that night, a big gray sedan careened around a downtown corner, a squad car in hot pursuit. The driver of the sedan was an expert, a top professional whose racing career had been cut short when he was convicted of deliberately running over a member of a rival pit crew during the Gotham Grand Prix. Now the driver made his living moving contraband from one city to another. In the trunk of the sedan was a full set of plates to print counterfeit twenty-dollar bills. Most of the time, the driver never had to display his skills. Usually he could manage the delivery without a problem. "Somebody must have tipped off the cops," he thought. "Not that it will do them any good."

In his skilled hands, the gray sedan was a precision instrument—under its nondescript exterior, it was built to the specifications of a race machine, a gross overmatch against conventional police cars. With every block, his lead on his police pursuers widened. Suddenly another car joined the chase—an unmarked car with two detectives in the front seat. The driver smiled—with a steering wheel in his hands, he was more than a match for a bunch of ham-fisted amateurs.

The gray sedan took the next corner in a controlled four-wheel drift, scraping the squad car off against a parked delivery van. The glass-and-metal sound was unmistakable—music to the driver's ears. He stabbed the brake, executing a perfect J-turn as the unmarked car shot past him helplessly. A quick turn into an alley, and the driver vanished from sight. If driving seventy miles an hour through a passage with only a couple of inches' clearance on each side caused him any concern, it didn't show on his face.

Another ten minutes brought the driver to the edge of the warehouse district. He smiled in smug satisfaction—once he got into that maze of narrow streets, there wouldn't be a cop on the planet who could give him a run for his money. The driver glanced into the rearview mirror, checking for the headlights of pursuers. The mirror was empty. But . . . the driver cocked his ears, listening. Was that a car engine he heard in the distance? No . . . it was too high-pitched, more of a whine than a roar. Just like a . . .

The driver snapped into full alert. He recognized the sound now. There was only one vehicle in all of Gotham that used a turbine for power.

"Damn!" the driver hissed under his breath. He stomped the gas pedal, instinctively correcting the car as it fishtailed on the wet asphalt. The gray sedan launched powerfully, heading for the cobblestone pavement that ran parallel to the river. The driver leaned over the wheel, no longer relaxed. "One more fall and I'm history," he muttered to himself, images of the notorious Hellgate Prison looming in his mind. His last stay had been unpleasant—he wasn't going back quietly. The gray sedan skittered over the cobblestones as the driver urged it onward. He stole a quick glance at the mirror. It was still dark. Wait! Then the driver saw it—a tiny red dot. He knew what it meant—a warning that the Batmobile was in pursuit. A warning to pull over and surrender.

"Fat chance!" the driver muttered under his breath. "Whoever he is, he's still human. And if he's human, I can outdrive him."

The driver saw his chance—a long S-curve just ahead. He dove for the apex of the first turn, inviting his pursuer to pull alongside. The Batmobile accepted the invitation, rushing up on the right of the sedan. "A little closer," the driver said to himself. "Just a little closer . . . now!" The driver mashed the brake pedal at the same time as he cranked the wheel over hard to the left. The sedan's rear end came around like a steel whip . . . but the Batmobile wasn't there—it had braked just before the driver did, moving in right behind the sliding rear end of the gray sedan.

Centrifugal force did the rest—the driver had no chance to scream before the gray sedan slid off the curve and into the black water.

"Funny thing," one of the Rescue Squad divers said to another. "He didn't hang around."

"What are you talking about?" the other asked.

"Oh, yeah. I forgot—you're new here. I've been out

on plenty of these. Every once in a while, some crook thinks he can take on the Batmobile, and he ends up in the drink. But every other time, the Batman hangs around, sort of. Just to make sure the guy's okay, I guess.''

"Well, we fished him out, didn't we?''

"Sure. I mean, he wasn't really in that much trouble, not with the Batman calling us in even before the crash. But . . . I don't know, it seems different this time. He didn't even look back.''

Still later that night, a pair of nurses were walking from the hospital exit to the parking lot. They had just finished a double shift—happy to be done, but almost too tired to care. They were practically to their car when a man wearing a red ski mask blocked their path.

"Drop your pocketbooks!'' he commanded, brandishing a machete.

The blonde nurse tossed her purse on the ground. "Just take it and go away,'' she said calmly. "We don't want any trouble.''

The robber moved forward, but as he bent to pick up the purse, the brunette nurse threw a side kick at his head. The robber jumped back just in time to avoid the kick, and the brunette fell to the ground.

"You shouldn't have tried that,'' he snarled. "Now it's going to cost you more than money.'' He raised the machete just as the blonde let out a bloodcurdling scream. The robber hesitated only a split second, but it was enough time for the brunette to scramble to her feet.

"Spread out, Bonnie," she said. "He can't take us both at once."

"Tough broads, aren't you?" the robber sneered. "Too bad nobody could hear you scream way out here." He watched their faces for the signs of fear that were so intoxicating to him, but the nurses both stood transfixed, staring at something behind him. "You expect me to fall for that old . . ."

All the nurses saw was a flash of movement. All they heard was a loud, dry *snaaap!* but they both knew what it meant even before the robber's words were choked off into an anguished shriek. The robber fell to the ground as the machete dropped from his nerveless fingers. His useless right arm dangled limply. His face was white with pain.

"Compound fracture," the blonde nurse said to her friend. "I'll stay here to watch him—you go get security."

"I don't want to . . ." her friend started to say.

"Go ahead. I'll be fine. This one isn't going to give anyone any trouble . . . not for a long time."

Dawn was breaking as the two nurses told their story to a detective.

"You're sure?" the detective asked.

"We're sure," the brunette nurse answered. "It was the Batman. We both saw him."

"You're saying that Batman . . . the *Batman* snapped this guy's arm like a twig and just took off?"

"Yes," the blonde nurse said, an edge of annoyance in her voice. "Yes, for the third time."

"Okay, ladies, okay," the detective surrendered. "I'm not saying you didn't see what you saw." He scratched his head in puzzlement. "It just don't sound like the Batman, that's all."

"It's not enough," he said to himself. Over and over again, like a mantra. "It's not enough," the Batman said. "It's not enough," his alter ego echoed.

"Sir?" Albert asked, raising an eyebrow.

"Huh?" Bruce Wayne replied, as though awakening from a deep sleep. "Sorry, Alfred. I must have been day-dreaming."

"With all respect, Master Bruce, I don't think so. You have been repeating the same thing over and over again for some time now. You keep saying, 'It's not enough.' Are you . . . ?"

"I'm fine, Alfred. I just . . . think it's time to make some decisions."

"May I be of help, sir?"

"I don't think so, old friend. On the other hand, I

guess you've *already* been of help. Of great help, in fact. Do you remember, when I was a boy, how you cautioned me against trying to solve a problem without adequate data?"

"Of course, Master Bruce. But I don't see how . . ."

"I'm going out, Alfred. I'm going out to gather the data I need."

"Then you'll be needing the Batmobile, sir?"

"No, Alfred. This is one investigation where I can learn more as . . ."

"As yourself, sir?"

"I'm not sure," Bruce replied, a note of ephemeral sadness running like a dark thread through his voice.

"You're serious?" Debra Kane asked into the phone. "You really want to go on rounds with me?"

"That's *exactly* what I want," Bruce Wayne said. "If you don't believe it would hinder . . ."

"It's not that," Debra Kane replied. "I'm just . . . surprised. Nobody ever asked to do that before. I'm not even sure it's okay. I mean, the agency might not want other people along. You know, confidentiality and all that."

"Don't worry," Bruce Wayne assured her. "I'll make sure you have all the necessary permissions in your hand before tomorrow night. How's that?"

"I'll look forward to seeing you, Mr. Wayne," Debra Kane said. "Tomorrow night then? Around six?"

"I'll be there," Bruce Wayne promised.

"Why would Bruce Wayne want to make the rounds with some social worker?" the mayor asked, looking across his wide oak desk at Police Commissioner Gordon.

"He said he wants to see where resources are needed," the commissioner replied. "And he wants to see for himself."

"Doesn't sound like him, does it? I mean . . . he's kind of a playboy, isn't he? Doesn't do much of anything but go to parties."

"Some of those parties are fund-raisers," the commissioner said pointedly. "If he wants to do it, that's good enough for me. Of course, his lawyers have already prepared a full waiver and release. If something happens to him while he's out there, we won't be held responsible."

"Well . . . I suppose it's not inappropriate for a public-spirited individual to see how his tax dollars are spent."

"I appreciate your cooperation," the commissioner said. "And I know Bruce will, too."

"Debra, you'll never believe who's out at the front desk. Asking for *you!*" the chubby, sweet-faced receptionist whispered breathlessly into the phone.

"If it's Bruce Wayne, just send him back, Clarissa."

"All *right*, girl. One super-rich hunk, coming up!" The receptionist looked up to catch Bruce Wayne's eye.

"You can go right through that door," she said. "Follow the blue arrow to room 109, okay?"

"Thank you," Bruce said.

Clarissa's heart melted. She cast her big brown eyes skyward and said, "Okay, when is it going to be *my* turn, huh?"

The door to room 109 was ajar. Bruce Wayne peeked in. Debra spotted him and waved him to an empty chair next to her desk. "I'll be off in a minute," she mouthed silently, then returned to her phone conversation.

She took rapid notes with a felt-tip pen for a while, asking only "prompt" questions herself: "When did it happen? How do you know? Did she see a doctor?"

Finally she put down the phone. "I'm glad you could come," she said, a reserved look on her face.

Bruce Wayne smiled. "I wanted to . . . get the facts. Some facts, anyway."

"To see where your tax dollars are going?"

"Would that be so bad?" he asked seriously. "Wouldn't you want tax-paying citizens to have some idea of what they're buying?"

"I . . . suppose," Debra replied. "It's just that people's priorities are so . . ."

"Selfish?"

"This isn't charity we do here, Mr. Wayne, despite what you may think. Please don't confuse Child Protective Services with Welfare—they're not the same."

"Well then, I've learned something already," he said, smiling again.

Debra didn't smile back, but her face lost some of its primness as she regarded the man sitting across from her. "You understand that there's two parts to my job. I have to investigate new cases, and I have to check on the progress of some older ones. Do you have any preference as to which you'd like to see?''

"Both," the handsome man said.

The dull gray sedan was undistinguished except for GOTHAM SOCIAL SERVICES stenciled on its front doors. It made its way crosstown, Debra Kane at the wheel.

"Have you ever been to the Randall Street Projects?" she asked.

"Not as Bruce Wayne," the man next to her thought to himself. Aloud he simply answered, "I don't believe so."

"If you'd ever been there, you'd remember it. It was built in the sixties. Social engineering in the very real sense. The idea was to provide affordable housing for working people."

"Are you saying that was a bad idea?"

"No. In fact, the *idea* was great. But the execution was lacking. The people who designed it had no idea what working people needed . . . what their children needed. They were so excited about their *concepts*," she said sarcastically, "that they forgot people actually lived in what they built."

"I still don't understand," he said.

"Take a look," Debra Kane replied, turning the wheel so the car could enter the parking lot.

Bruce Wayne turned his head, but it was the Batman's trained eyes that scanned the Project, registering details, assimilating information. The Project was a series of slab-faced brick buildings, twenty stories high. The outside stairways were faced with chicken wire to prevent children from falling—it served the same purpose for the drunks and addicts randomly spewed about on the steps. Security lights blazed from the high corners. The front doors were buried under dozens of coats of graffiti. Cardboard covered many of the windows. A giant smokestack belched black fumes from the incinerator.

"It looks like a . . . prison," he said finally.

"That's what it *feels* like, too," Debra Kane replied. "Come on."

She walked briskly across the parking lot, seemingly oblivious to the catcalls and wolf whistles. The front doors stood slightly open at the center, their locks long since smashed off. Inside the foyer, Bruce saw the mailboxes had suffered the same treatment. The elevator had a hand-scrawled OUT OF ORDER sign pasted to its door.

"I wouldn't ride it anyway," Debra Kane said. "It's not safe."

"Because it might fall?" Bruce Wayne asked.

"That too," she said cryptically. "We need 16-B. I hope you're in shape."

The stairs were littered with refuse. Bags of garbage were strewn carelessly around.

"Why don't they put their garbage in the incinerator?" Bruce asked.

"Most of the time, it isn't working," Debra told him. "At least they're not airmailing it."

"Airmailing?"

"Throwing it out the window," she said, a slight smile on her lips. "You don't ever want to walk in the area behind the Projects . . . trust me."

By the ninth floor, Debra Kane was breathing with more difficulty, but climbing at the same pace she started with. "Are you all right?" she asked her companion. "I'm sure you're not used to this."

"I'll . . . be okay," he replied, careful to give the impression that his aerobic capacity was being taxed by the climb.

When they reached the sixteenth floor, Debra held up one hand, palm out. Bruce Wayne halted, his eyes questioning. "I have to get my breath back," she explained. "When you go into one of these places, you can't be out of breath."

"Because . . . ?"

"Because you may end up in a pitched battle," she said calmly. "You never know what's behind one of these doors."

"In the Projects?" he asked.

"Anywhere," she said flatly.

Debra walked briskly down the hall to 16-B and rapped sharply on the door. After a minute, the door was opened a few inches, the way barred by a length of chain. A woman's face showed through, as worn and tired as the floor of a bus depot.

"What is it?" she asked.

"Child Protective Services, ma'am," Debra said.

"I didn't call no—"

"Yes ma'am, I understand. Still, we *were* notified, and . . ."

"Well, who called you, then?"

"That's confidential, ma'am. If we could just come in and sit down, maybe we could . . ."

"Get away from that door!" A male voice: loud, aggressive, alcohol-blurred. The owner of the voice filled the doorway. He pulled the chain loose, opened the door wider. He was a broad-chested man with the body of a former athlete recently gone to seed. "What the hell do you want?" he demanded of Debra.

"As I was just explaining, sir. We're from Child Protective Services and . . ."

"You saying one of the brats called you?" he challenged.

"No, sir, I'm not. I *am* telling you this: we received notice of a situation here, a situation we are mandated to investigate. We need to speak with you, and with your children."

"And what if I say you can't?" he sneered, fixing the social worker with his most intimidating stare—the same stare that had backed men down in gin mills throughout the neighborhood.

"Then we'll return with the police," Debra replied calmly, meeting his eyes.

Ten seconds passed.

"Ah, do what you want," the man said, turning his back and walking away from Debra.

An hour later, a pretty ten-year-old named Mary Lou was explaining how she got the inflamed black eye that had first attracted the attention of a school nurse. "I didn't want him to hit Scotty," she said. "Scotty's just a baby— he could be hurt real bad."

"Does he hit Scotty a lot?" Debra asked.

"Not . . . a *lot*, I guess. I don't know."

"Does he hit Scotty every day?"

"Sometimes," the child said. "When he cries, or if he spills something, or when he plays too loud. You know . . ."

"Does Daddy hit anybody else?" Debra asked.

"He hits everybody," the child said, obviously puzzled by such a stupid question.

"You heard enough?" the man of the house said, lurching around the corner to the bedroom where Debra was questioning the child.

"I think so," Debra said, closing her notebook.

"What did *she* tell you?" the man asked, pointing at his daughter.

"We'll discuss that later," Debra said crisply.

"What did you say?" the man demanded, leaning menacingly over his daughter. "Answer me!"

"Nothing, Daddy! I . . ."

The man backhanded the child, sailing her backward over the small bed. Debra jumped up, placing her body between the little girl and her father. The man whom Debra thought of as Bruce Wayne moved so quickly that he seemed to simply materialize at the man's side, one comforting hand on the man's neck.

"We're going in the other room," he said to Debra. "Just to get ourselves calmed down. Isn't that right?" he said to the man.

All the man felt was pain—lancing white needles of pain. All the man knew was that when he nodded his head quietly, the pain went away.

Later, sitting downstairs in the car, Bruce Wayne asked, "What's going to happen to them?"

"It's a close decision," Debra said. "There's no question but that he beats the children. And his wife as well. They all say he isn't usually like this . . . only when he's drinking. And since he lost his job, he's been drinking a lot."

"Won't the kids go to a foster home?" the billionaire wanted to know.

"It's not that simple," she replied. "First of all, the most important thing for Mary Lou is not to be separated from her little brother . . . with foster home placement, that can't be guaranteed. And, more to the point, neither child wants to leave. They want Daddy to be like he was once, before he lost his job and started drinking so much . . . but they don't want to leave. I know it looks ugly to you, but it's really a Category One case.''

"Category One?"

"Yes," Debra said. "Essentially, it means people who are doing inadequate parenting. Sometimes they just don't know how to *be* a parent. How would a thirteen-year-old girl know how to be a mother?—she's not done with being a child. Other times people know, but they're so overwhelmed by their own problems they don't think about anyone else. Take that man upstairs. I grant you, he's no prize package. But his real problem is unemployment. And that's not something we can fix.''

"What *can* you fix?" he asked.

Debra searched his face for any trace of sarcasm. Finding none, she answered, "We'll file a petition so that the family becomes entitled to services. Alcoholism counseling for the father, periodic checks to be sure he isn't hitting the children anymore, family counseling for the whole unit, individual treatment for the children. There's *lots* of things we can do," she said sadly. "But it's never enough.''

"I . . . talked to him," Bruce Wayne said. "In the other room.''

"I noticed," Debra said. "You have a real calming way about you. I was just amazed at how quiet he got.''

"He kept saying, 'They used to respect me,' " Bruce Wayne told her. "That's what he kept saying. Over and over.''

"Yes," Debra said, her tone of voice making it clear

she did not share Bruce's sense of amazement. "He was . . . distraught. He knows what he's doing is lousy. And he feels lousy about it. It's as though he's lost control. Nothing that happens in his life has anything to do with him anymore. He's no longer the breadwinner, the . . . *man.* I feel bad for him. But I feel worse for the children. And, if something isn't done, for *their* children as well."

"Is that why you went?" Bruce asked.

"Went? Went where?"

"To the . . . party, I guess you'd call it. At the Gotham Museum. Did you think some of the people there could—?"

"I don't know *what* I was thinking," Debra Kane replied. "At first, I thought it would be . . . I don't know, *exciting,* maybe. All those rich and famous people. Besides, I heard they have great food at those things. But as soon as I looked around, I just couldn't *stand* it. All those smug, pompous, self-congratulatory people. As if their *money* made them important. I knew I didn't belong there—"

"Like I did?" Bruce Wayne finished for her.

Debra felt her face blushing, but she met his eyes. "That *is* what I thought," she said. "I still don't know why you went out with me—I mean, out on *rounds* with me," she corrected, blushing even more deeply.

"But it's all right if I do it again?" he asked.

"If you've got the stomach, I've got the time," Debra Kane answered.

Eight nights later, at the end of a ten-hour shift, Bruce Wayne and Debra Kane sat across from each other in a back booth of the otherwise unnamed OPEN ALL NIGHT DINER. Debra was on her third cup of black coffee. Bruce was still nursing his first glass of tea.

"Is it always like this?" he asked. His face, usually a fleshy mask of blandness, was creased with the pain he had seen so many times in the past several nights.

"Sure. It gets more or less intense depending on a whole lot of things, but this is about normal."

"Normal? Being beaten by a drunk? Whipped with an electric cord? Scalded down to third-degree burns? Left alone for four days with nothing to eat except dry cereal? Sodomized by an uncle?"

"All of that and more," Debra said.

"It doesn't seem . . ."

"Possible?"

"Human. It doesn't seem human."

"It's classically human, Bruce," Debra replied, having dropped the "Mr. Wayne" days ago . . . while yelling at him to call an ambulance for the baby who had been shaken into permanent brain damage. "Being a parent means a lot more than giving birth. And a lot of people haven't gone much beyond that."

"Remember the first case I went on with you? You said it was a Category One case, remember?"

"Yes."

"What are the other categories?"

Debra took another sip of her coffee, choosing her words carefully. "Do you remember the one on Baxter Street?"

"Yes. How could I forget? That woman was insane! Imagine, thinking she could bake the devilment out of a little child and . . ."

"Put him in the oven to do it?" Debra finished. "That's Category Two. Crazy. Genuinely crazy, like paranoid schizophrenic. Or obsessive-compulsive. Or any other diagnosis you want."

"Can you do anything with them?"

"With some? Sure. With others, no way."

"The man in that nice apartment? The one right off the drive?"

"Yes?" Debra asked, a quick look of disgust flashing across her face.

"He was Category Two, then?"

"No, Bruce. No, he wasn't."

"But . . . incest. I mean . . . with his own daughter. His own little girl. Are you telling me that isn't sick?"

"That's just what I *am* telling you. Like most people who have never seen it firsthand, you have *sick* confused with *sickening*. What you saw there was a classic Category Three—people who hurt children for their own pleasure and their own profit."

"But . . . I'm confused. He said he . . . loved her. And he was just . . ."

"Love?" Debra's voice dripped venom, her eyes alive with anger. "Sure, he *loved* that child—the same way he would *love* a good steak—for the pleasure it gives him. Nothing else. That poor little girl will carry that ugly weight the rest of her life. It doesn't matter what laws you choose to govern your life. They could be the laws of God, the laws of Nature, or the laws of Mankind. Incest violates them *all.* It's not sick, Bruce, it's evil."

She abruptly got up from the table and walked out. By the time he paid the check and joined her outside, her face was set and composed. "I'm sorry," she said. "I know you mean well. But I really can't talk about this any more tonight."

"Can I . . . come along again sometime?"

"You really want to do that?"

"I really do."

Debra nodded slowly. Then she put the car into gear and aimed it for the CPS agency.

They wouldn't let him sleep. The children gnawed at the edge of his consciousness, scraping his nerve endings raw, challenging his sense of justice.

Bruce Wayne couldn't take it.

The Batmobile shot out of its underground bunker—
an avenger's arrow, seeking a target. Behind the cowl, the
Batman's eyes smoldered. His jaw was locked into a flat-
mouthed grimace, but his breathing was slow and controlled. The Batmobile ran on its shrouded lower lights
as it glided through traffic. The driver of an eighteen-
wheeler felt the ominous shape slip by, but before he
could crane his neck to look closer, the night-shark had
vanished, leaving only the turbine's mournful whistle in
its wake.

"Ah, it's only the wind," the trucker comforted himself, suppressing an involuntary shudder.

And maybe it was . . . a *dangerous* wind for those who
walked on the wrong side of the law.

The crime fighter checked his view screen, rapidly
punching in the coordinates for the Excelsior, an uptown
luxury building owned by Wayne Enterprises. All clear. A
gloved finger flicked a toggle switch, and the building's
underground garage door opened. The Batmobile
entered smoothly, but instead of parking, the long black
machine drove toward the back wall. A slot in the wall
opened, and the Batmobile disappeared from view. An
elevator took the vehicle and its occupant to the subbase-
ment. Moving entirely in darkness, the Batman maneuvered the machine until it was pointing up a slight incline.

The Batman climbed out and felt along the wall until
his fingers touched a flat button set almost flush. A smaller
door opened, and the Batman slipped through it. He
stepped into a one-man elevator. As soon as he closed the
door, the elevator shot upward. At its apex, it opened
automatically. The Batman found himself on the roof, just
inside a giant greenhouse maintained by the occupant of
the penthouse suite.

Nobody ever saw that occupant—all the tenants ever observed was a steady stream of support personnel: maids, gardeners, occasionally a caterer. The tenants didn't ask direct questions—such conduct was considered beneath the dignity of the city's elite—but even their most discreet inquiries never seemed to produce any answers of substance.

"I swear I think the place is inhabited by ghosts," one matron said to another.

"They *are* doing wonderful things with trust funds these days," her neighbor replied.

In fact, the building was one of the Batman's strike-bases. The Batmobile could be made to appear or disappear at will. The rooftop was all the access the crime fighter needed to the rest of the city. And if he was injured, the penthouse had a full complement of medical and surgical supplies . . . as well as a panic button that would bring Alfred on the run.

Now it was time to hunt.

The apartment was right off Gotham Drive, just inside the diamond-spine of the great city. The Batman watched from one rooftop away. Watched the light go off as the apartment dropped into darkness. Something he didn't understand pulled him magnetically to that spot. He knew who lived there—the incest offender who told Debra Kane how much he loved his little girl. But what was he doing . . .

A tiny red dot popped into view. The Batman narrowed his gaze across the gap. Yes. A cigarette. The child's father was out on his balcony, looking down at the city, enjoying a last smoke before going to bed. Going to bed with . . .

The Batman felt a trembling inside his chest, a hot, burning sensation behind his eyes. How easy it would be to just . . .

"No!" he said to himself. "I took an oath. The authorities already know about him. I can't just . . ."

The crime fighter stayed at his perch, rooted as though turned into petrified wood, standing long after the creature had finished his cigarette and gone inside.

"It's not enough," he whispered aloud.

Twenty minutes later, a burglar's luck turned bad. The Batman spotted his prey just as the second-story man was exiting an apartment window, a sack of loot over his shoulder. "Drop it!" the Batman commanded.

The burglar was a three-time loser. "I'm not going back to prison," he muttered as he pulled a pistol from inside his coat.

That's when his luck turned worse. The Batman stepped inside the burglar's gun arm, sweeping upward in a perfectly executed swing-away. The pistol flew from the burglar's hand. Seeing his hope of escape falling away, he ignored the Batman's outstretched hand and grabbed for the gun instead. He came up short and tumbled out into space, still reaching. The Batman instantly dove forward, sliding on his stomach, back arched like a cobra, grabbing for the burglar's foot as the thief disappeared over the edge. The Batman's desperate slide carried his upper body past the roof's edge but he was still a heartbeat late. Holding on only with his feet, he peered into the dark, but there was nothing to see. Suddenly the falling burglar screamed—his last words were a curse, echoing all the way down the concrete canyon.

The Batman slowly pulled himself back to the safety of the roof. And as he did so, he felt within him, deep in his soul, a tremor that was new to him.

He didn't like the feeling.

"Alfred," Bruce Wayne said the next day, "would you call up the *Current Whereabouts Program* on the computer?"

"Certainly, Master Bruce. Do we have a subset?"

"Yes. Try *Convicts in Custody* first—it's a much quicker run."

"Whatever you say, sir. But wouldn't—?"

"The man I'm looking for will still be inside," Bruce Wayne gently interrupted. "No doubt about it."

"May I ask who . . . ?"

"The Middleman."

"I'm sure you're correct, Master Bruce. Let me run a check, and I'll be back to you with a printout in just a short time."

"Thanks, Alfred."

"Not at all," the faithful Alfred replied, his face a

study in serenity—a face that effectively hid a growing sense of unease about the man who only came alive as the Batman.

Hellgate Prison was a little more than a two-hour drive from the modern glitter of Gotham. In appearance, however, it was light-years away. Resting in a natural valley surrounded by gentle rolling hills, it resembled nothing so much as a giant meteor that had slammed into the earth with sufficient force to create a depression.

Restricted only to those criminals considered extremely dangerous or an escape risk, Hellgate was the garbage can of the criminal justice system, a max-max institution without pretense. Hellgate was a cage. A cage for beasts.

At ground level, a visitor would see only the huge ornamental iron gate that originally gave the prison its name. As if to emphasize that this was the only way out of the huge, glowering prison, the gate was set between massive stone walls. Four feet thick and twenty feet high, the walls dominated the eye and symbolized the reality— those inside were shut away from society as completely as any exile.

But from his vantage point near the peak of one of the surrounding hills, the Batman could see inside. Flicking the scope to night vision with a gloved thumb, the crime fighter studied his target. On wide-angle, the scope illuminated the coils of concertina wire looping the top of the walls and the guard towers where sharpshooters awaited the rare opportunity to demonstrate their skills.

The lens took in the artificial moat at the outer base of the walls—a moat filled with specially trained members of the prison K-9 Corps.

There hadn't been a successful escape from Hellgate in two decades. In that time, almost three hundred escapes were attempted. With few exceptions, all the convicts were captured before they could scale the wall. The exceptions died trying.

The Batman had dedicated his life to fighting crime, a commitment that required a deep understanding of the enemy. Surveillance was not enough—neither was mastery of underworld slang, nor a network of informants. All of those resources were utilized to the fullest, but even their combined total did not add up to a sufficient tactical edge in the endless battle. The crime fighter had gone one step further in his study of the enemy: after years and years of concentrated exposure, the Batman could literally *think* like a criminal. He could *become* a criminal in his mind—tuning in to another frequency and following the beam to its source. It was that ability, more than any other, which made the Batman the most convincing—and successful—undercover operative ever known to penetrate the underworld.

"I can't get over that wall," the Batman spoke in his mind, *becoming* a desperate convict, looking through the convict's eyes, looking through the bars to the outside world. "Even if I could get past the gun towers, even if I could get through the razor wire, the dogs would eat me alive."

The Batman knew how the escape-bound convict applies himself with a focus and dedication that would do credit to a nuclear physicist. He thinks of nothing else.

Day after day, he poses one hypothesis after another, field-testing the equations with his eyes and ears.

And with the history of those who had gone before him. Gone *down*.

The Batman dropped deeper into the mind of the escape-obsessed prisoner. He slowed his heartbeat to open the channel, not forcing, letting it happen. Waiting with the patience of a stone. Asking: how can I get out of here?

Images flickered on his brain-screen.

Bribery? Corruption? Blackmail?

All possibilities, none of them a sure thing.

Parole? Commutation? Pardon?

The Batman's convict-mind chuckled mirthlessly. Fat chance, his mind sneered.

What, then? Surrender? Just quietly serve your sentence?

This time, the chuckle was a sarcastic sneer.

There must be . . . *Yes!*

The Batman snapped out of his convict persona in a flash, his mind immediately refocused to the hunt. He quickly tapped a series of microbuttons in the Batmobile's overhead console, watching the view-screen intently as the image shifted. A small green LED blinked rapidly. A message appeared at the bottom right of the screen:

Probe/SONAR Engagement in Progress. Please wait . . .

A long narrow panel opened at the rear of the Batmobile. A tiny black tube appeared in the opening. Then it launched into the night, popping open flexible metallic wings as it glided toward the prison. Two more of the probes followed. The screen message showed:

Triangulation in Progress. Please wait . . .

The screen showed a flat grid on which the image of the prison was superimposed. The three tiny probes appeared as dots on the grid. The Batman made gentle adjustments of the dots with a joystick on the center console. He nodded in satisfaction just as the screen message confirmed:

Triangulation in Place // Select Dimension

A gloved hand tapped buttons in the overhead console.

Selected: Depth // Is this correct?

The Batman tapped a key to confirm.

Imaging. Please wait . . .

In less than thirty seconds, the screen showed a diagram of the prison in profile. The Batman leaned forward as the three sonar-probes converged to show him an ultrasound image of the ground below. He slowly exhaled as the screen revealed what he had suspected.

A tunnel. A deep, reinforced tunnel running below Hellgate Prison. The probes showed the tunnel had started somewhere in the Hospital Wing, ran parallel to the prison until it veered sharply left, avoiding the Exercise Yard and the Administration Building, heading for the back wall. The Batman scanned the screen, quickly translating the symbols to numbers—the tunnel was approximately twelve feet short of the wall.

The crime fighter worked the joystick. The computer analyzed the probe's information and worked out the answer he sought. The prison wall was six feet deep—the tunnel must be below that depth.

The Batman sat quietly for a moment, briefly savoring the new information. Then he went to work, asking the computer a series of questions to be answered by new data inputs.

Estimate: time needed to complete tunnel

600 to 1900 man-hours

Depending on?

Weather conditions, implements used, individual strength of diggers

The crime fighter mused over the information. No matter how many convicts were in on the tunnel plot, only one or at most two could dig at any one time—anyone planning to use the tunnel would have a long time to wait.

But inside Hellgate, time was never in short supply.

The Batman once again tapped some console keys, his eyes on the screen.

Sylvester Sistrunk

a/k/a THE MIDDLEMAN

W/M · BR-BLD/BLU · 12/25/51(44) · 72/209 · Gotham PL § 100/105/115/165/170/185/225/230/450

Translate last:

Penal Law Offenses: Criminal Solicitation, Conspiracy, Criminal Facilitation, Theft, Forgery, Fraud, Gambling Offenses, Prostitution Offenses, Disposal of Stolen Property, Money Laundering

Open /Prostitution Offenses/

One Martin Despain, a known pimp with 5 prior felony convictions, obtained a license to operate a fitness gym. In fact, the premises were used as a "massage parlor." Most of the information furnished on the license application was fictitious. Sistrunk arranged a meeting between Despain and Charles Montaingue, an employee of Gotham Licensing Board. Despain bribed Montaingue. The license was granted. It was later discovered that Sistrunk was paid $20,000 by Despain to set up the meeting, and also $3,000 by Montaingue as his "broker's commission."

Personal contact with Prostitution Offenses?

None. Note: subject has no personal contact with ANY crime, hence his a/k/a . . . the Middleman

Sentence serving?

Individual or cumulative?

Total

Total, all crimes, all counts = 1,588 years.

Actual time to parole eligibility?

7 years, 4 months, 11 days

The Batman examined and reexamined the data. One more question for the computer.

Location . . . narrowcast

Hellgate Prison, Wing #5, Tier #3, Cell #1

Image in

Scanning. Please wait . . .

A side view of the prison came up on the screen. The view shifted on its axis, the better to display the wing that housed the Middleman. A blinking red arrow pointed at a cell located on the top floor at the far corner. The Batman used the joystick to dolly in. He studied the image for a moment, then typed:

Probe // Switch to Video

Switching Please wait . . .

The screen image changed from diagrammatic representation to live video. The Batman zoomed in on his target, commanding the probes to their tightest close-up. The barred window to the Middleman's cell filled the screen, but inside was nothing but murky darkness. The Batman glanced quickly at the digital clock in the upper right corner of the video screen—01:04:53.8—a little past one in the morning. The Batman nodded to himself and tapped the keys again.

Probe // Switch to Thermal

Switching. Please wait . . .

After a few seconds, the screen went fluorescent, the images ranging from deep blue to vibrant yellow. The Batman adjusted the probes until he had a fix on the cell's interior. The elongated red splotch was the Middleman, obviously lying on his bunk, the flash of yellow was his head. The Batman studied the data as he brought the image as close as the probes' triangulation would permit. Just one more piece of information was needed.

Conscious state?

Sleep

Depth?

REM

So the Middleman was deep asleep. Dreaming, in fact. Now all he had to know was . . .

The computer beeped. The Batman's eyes turned toward the screen.

ALERT! Additional Data Available / Request?

Y

Perry Trauma Scale available. Run?

Y

The Batman's eyes were riveted to the screen. The Perry Trauma Scale was named for Dr. B. D. Perry, short-listed for next year's International Contribution to Humanity Award for his groundbreaking research into the biochemistry of trauma. Dr. Perry's thesis was that deeply traumatized children process information differently than those not so afflicted. One example is the "startle reaction" familiar to every social worker—the child who cringes when a hand is raised to wave "hello" is a child who has learned a raised hand means a blow. Sometimes that learning is buried so deeply that no amount of contrary information will change the reaction to the same stimuli. Perry's work was still in progress, but his Trauma Scale, which measured *past* trauma recorded, was now used in all child abuse screenings. As the Trauma Scale ranking is obtained by reading brain-wave patterns while the subject is in a sleep state, much of the wind had gone out of the sails of the "false allegations" movement. The new program had just been installed into the Batcomputer, and the Batman was eager to test it.

He waited patiently. Then, superimposed over the thermal image, the screen read:

Perry Trauma Scale: B/71/C/NR

The crime fighter quickly translated. "B" meant the second distinct life stage, somewhere between two and four years of age, depending upon the individual. "71" was the degree of severity. "C" indicated chronic, as opposed to episodic. And "NR" stood for "not repressed."

Something had happened to the Middleman when he was a young child—something deeply traumatic. And whatever it was, it was still on his mind.

The Batman leaned back and touched a button below the steering wheel. The Batmobile's canopy slid open with a faint *whooosh!* The Batman climbed out and looked down at the prison, shading his eyes from the moonlight. After a long minute, he reached back inside the Batmobile and hit the switches to retrieve the probes, a falconer recalling his birds. Once they were back inside their cages, the Batman opened a large panel and pulled out what looked like a backpack harness. The straps were cleverly designed to precisely match his costume. He slipped the harness over his shoulders, taking care that his cape hung on the outside, completely concealing the backpack from view.

The Batman touched a transmitter on his utility belt and the Batmobile's pneumatic pistons pushed the canopy

closed—in that position, the vehicle was virtually invulner-
able to attack.

Then the Batman stepped to the very edge of a nearby
precipice, spread his wings, and dove into the night.

The Batman used the titanium-reinforced "veins" in his
cape to adjust for maximum glide. He rode the thermals
smoothly, vectoring in. When he was satisfied that he was
well launched, the Batman touched off the mini-jet engine
strapped to his back. The engine was crafted for maximum
portability—it didn't have the thrust to lift a man airborne,
only enough to sustain flight once in the air.

The Batman swept past the gun towers in a high arc,
positioning himself precisely. The mini-jet engine had no
capacity to reverse-thrust—it was necessary to turn it off
completely in order to land. The Batman made two more
passes, familiarizing himself with wind currents and checking for downdraft. He aimed himself upward, increased thrust, then extinguished the mini-jet at the peak
of his climb.

Using his cape as a modified parachute, the Batman
softly descended from the night sky, landing on the prison
roof in an acrobatic move no Olympic gymnast could
hope to imitate. He took another thirty seconds to orient
himself, taking care to insure that his presence was not
detected by the sweeping searchlights attached to the tops
of the gun towers. From his utility belt, the crime fighter
pulled a length of Batrope, a special combination of woven
fibers that had the flexibility of wire and the tensile
strength of a steel cable. He secured the Batrope on the

roof, then played out its length until he was standing at the edge. Then he allowed himself to fall forward, at the same time frog-kicking his legs so that when he reached the end of the cable he was suspended in resting-bat position right outside the Middleman's cell window.

A quick glance confirmed the Middleman was still asleep. From his utility belt, the Batman took a flat disc of clear plastic with a fine network of microwires running through it. He carefully peeled off the adhesive on one side and plastered it against the glass, just inside the heavy bars. The S&R disc, as it was known to Emergency Services personnel, was originally designed by the Batman to aid in search-and-rescue efforts. It functioned as a two-way voice amplifier. Placed against the outside wall of a mine shaft cave-in, it allowed the rescuers to actually hear the voices of those trapped inside. The back-and-forth communication not only speeded rescue, it gave off a steady supply of hope to all concerned. A separate transmitter allowed the rescuers to dial in the amount of amplification needed.

The Batman dialed the disc to its lowest setting, then whispered quietly:

"Sistrunk! Sistrunk, wake up!"

The sleeping figure stirred. A groggy voice said, "What the . . . ?"

"Over here," the Batman whispered. "By the window. Hurry up."

The Middleman sat up, rubbing his eyes. Seeing the blacked area in front of his cell window, he got up and walked toward it.

"Who's . . . *what!*" he exclaimed as he recognized the menacing form that had terrorized Gotham's criminals for so long hanging upside down outside his window.

"Keep quiet," the Batman whispered. "I came here to talk, that's all."

The Middleman gulped, but quickly regained the composure that had served him so well in his chosen profession. "Okay," he said. "Let's talk. As you can see, I certainly have time for it."

"You are a . . . facilitator, are you not?" the Batman asked. "You bring a willing buyer and a willing seller together?"

"That's me," the Middleman replied. "If you got something you want to move, you come to me. And if you got something you need, you come to me, too. All I do is put people together."

"This is off the record," the Batman whispered. "Do you understand what I mean by that?"

"Sure do," the Middleman replied, unable to keep the surprise from his voice. Every working criminal knew that when the Batman said something was "off the record," he would not give the information to the police. This was a necessary element of law enforcement—sometimes you let the little fish go in order to catch the sharks.

"You move contraband, yes?" the Batman queried. "Guns, narcotics, stolen art, jewelry."

"That, and more," the Middleman replied, a trace of pride in his whisper. "If there's a profit in it, *I'm* in it."

"That's why I came," the Batman said. "There's a question I want answered, and I'm willing to pay for it."

"I don't need money," the Middleman answered.

"It's not money—it's something much more valuable."

"What is it, then?"

"I will not say until you answer my questions. But I promise you what I say is true."

The Middleman scratched his chin, thinking. It was bizarre how much the underworld trusted its greatest enemy. Every criminal knew that the Batman's word was gold. In fact, any crook would be more likely to trust the Batman's word than that of his associates. "Fire away," the Middleman said.

"I . . . have been told," the Batman said quietly, "that there is profit . . . substantial profit . . . in child abuse. I have been told that, for some child abusers, there is both pleasure and profit in what they do. I can comprehend the . . . pleasure," the Batman said, almost choking on the word. "And I know there is a market for anything if you know where to look." Leaning closer, the Batman thrust his upside-down cowl closer to the glass. "Tell me where to look," he commanded.

The Middleman turned his back on the window. His face was a fright-mask of rage and terror. Sweat poured off his body. The tremors slowly decreased until he felt he had control of himself. He walked back over to his bunk, picked up his pack of cigarettes, stuck one in his mouth, and fired it up. Then he returned to the window. "I needed a smoke," he said, carefully cupping the tip so it couldn't be seen from outside—an old prison habit.

"Tell me," the Batman whispered urgently.

The Middleman took a deep drag of his cigarette. "There's lots of ways," he said, "but generally, they all come down to three. You can sell pictures of the kids; you can sell the kids' services; or you can just sell them outright."

"Explain," the Batman said, his whisper laced with just-below-critical-mass tension.

"Kiddie porn, there's a big market for that," the

Middleman said. "It's not that the market's so wide, it's that it's so deep. When one of those freaks—"

"Freaks?" the Batman interjected.

"Child molesters. Baby-rapers, pedophiles, whatever you want to call them," the Middleman responded. "To me, they're freaks, okay?"

"Go on," the Batman encouraged.

"Anyway, if any *one* of those freaks had enough money, he'd buy *all* the kiddie porn in the world, understand? Hell, the market's so good, there's people in it who ain't freaks themselves, you know what I mean?"

"No."

"Look, you think the big drug wholesalers are addicts? Of course not. Used to be that the people who manufactured kiddie porn was all freaks themselves, see? But not no more."

"What else?"

"Kiddie prostitution, that's another big one. Of course, it ain't as profitable as the porn stuff—kids get used up pretty quick in that life."

"And the last one?" the Batman asked.

"Well, it's kind of all connected," the Middleman said. "Some freaks ain't satisfied with just renting a kid. They want to buy one."

"To keep? Like a black market adoption?"

"Nah," the Middleman sneered. "To *use*, understand? Use any way they want. And when they're done, they just throw them away."

"You mean . . . ?"

"Yeah," the Middleman answered, a yellowish light flickering in the pupils of his eyes. "That's *exactly* what I mean."

The crime fighter's eyes burned through the bulletproof glass separating him from the Middleman. "There's a tunnel," he said distinctly, enunciating each syllable. "Under the prison. It's almost to the wall. The authorities know about it. Tomorrow is the day they're going to shut it down. Anyone caught in it at the time will be looking at a lot more years in here."

"I got it," the Middleman said. "Fair trade, too. Just like you said."

"I will—"

"Hold on!" the Middleman hissed. "Wait a minute. I got something to tell you."

The Batman didn't reply. He just remained in position, as still as the steel in the window bars.

"There's a guy. Out on the West Coast," the Middleman said. "He arranges tours. Sex tours. Out of the country. He takes people to places where it's legal to have sex with kids. Charges a fortune for it, too. And he's not the only one— sex tours are a huge business now."

"Does he—?"

"Let me tell it my way, all right?" the Middleman snapped. "His name is Drako, and you can always find him at a place called the Dragonfire Marina on the coast. His boat is the *Lollypop*. Tours cost from fifteen grand *up* . . . depending on what 'extras' you want. Tell him a guy called Lester Tuxley referred you."

"How can I find—?"

"Lester?" the Middleman replied. "Don't worry about Lester. He's in here. In another wing. Just came in, as a matter of fact. Just make real sure you tell Drako that you spoke with Lester *before* tonight, got it?"

"Yes. What can I—?"

"Nothing!" the Middleman cut in. "It's on the house."

A long minute passed between the two men. Then the Batman reached to pull the S&R disc from the bulletproof glass, preparing to go. Suddenly the Middleman placed his palm against the glass, his eyes beseeching. The Batman placed his gloved hand against the glass, palm out, covering the Middleman's own.

The Middleman whispered, "Make them pay!" Then he quickly took his hand away and turned his back.

The master criminal stood in that position for a dozen heartbeats, his whole body trembling.

When he turned around again, the Batman was gone.

As was his habit when the previous night's work had run almost to daylight, Bruce Wayne arose just past noon. Alfred, as professionally anticipatory as ever, entered the master suite with a full breakfast tray and the morning papers.

Bruce ate slowly, savoring the peacefulness of his surroundings. He perused the columns of newsprint through the filter of his trained eyes, automatically vacuuming anything related to crime. Nothing about the tunnel under Hellgate Prison, but this was not surprising—the Batman had called the information in to the authorities only a few hours ago.

Restless, Bruce Wayne quickly changed into a set of sweats and walked down to the complete gymnasium that was a unique feature of Wayne Manor. Unlike its counterparts, this particular gym was not designed for recreation. In fact, it resembled nothing so much as an obstacle course for advanced hand-to-hand combat training. Built into one of the rear corners of the mansion, the gym's ceiling sloped from a high of thirty-five to a low of three feet, offering numerous opportunities to practice skills ranging from rappeling to tunnel stalking. The lighting was infinitely adjustable, from blazing klieg fixtures to pitch-darkness. In one corner stood a long, boxlike structure. Inside the box was an intricate series of interlocking panels. The panels were all computer controlled. Set to RANDOM, they would move so as to continually (and unpredictably) alter the interior paths. The Batman used the entire apparatus to hone his tactile senses. One of his original martial arts instructors required students to learn blind-fighting to emphasize the need for *total* concentration. The sensei's gospel was that overdependence on any *one* of the senses was unacceptable in the complete warrior. The Batman agreed, and he had designed the Concentration Box to maintain his highly specialized skills at peak.

The Batman finished his workout with a unique cluster of exercises he had designed specifically around the needs of his lonely profession—a sequenced series combining yoga, free weights, and an extended martial arts kata that merged elements of aikido and karate.

The night-rider then flowed smoothly into a ninety-minute cool-down phase during which he practiced emotional disengagement, controlled dissociation, and psychokinetics.

Years and years of the most highly disciplined *foci* had raised the Batman's personal *ki* almost to the level of a force field—at least insofar as the criminal element was concerned. A major contributor to that legend was the

underworld's most efficient long-range killer, an appari-
tion known only as the Sniper. Nobody had ever seen the
Sniper in person, but his work spoke for itself. If the Sniper
took the job, you might as well buy a ticket to the autopsy.
He had been offered a one-million-dollar bounty on the
Batman by a loose syndicate of crime kingpins. The criminal coalition left word in the whisper-stream that they
wanted the Sniper to call. They were all assembled in a
hideout when the Sniper's reptilian voice hissed over the
phone lines.

"I don't want the job," he said over the speakerphone.
"I *pass*, understand?"

"Perhaps if we . . . ah, altered the . . . uh, compensa-
tion package?" one of the kingpins suggested slyly.

"You ain't *got* enough money," the Sniper said.
"There ain't enough money in the world. I tried him once,
about three years ago. Had him dead in my sights. And
when you're in *my* sights, you *are* dead, understand? I had
him full-frontal—that bat-symbol on his chest was right in
the crosshairs. I squeezed one off . . . perfect, like I always
do. He couldn't have heard me—I was almost a quarter
mile away. Working with a silencer, too. And I *missed*! He
didn't even move, and I missed. I don't know what the
Batman's got going for him—some kind of voodoo, I
heard once. But whatever he's got, I'm not going to try it
again."

Renaldo "Razorman" Ramoto's tale was similar. He
had the Batman cornered . . . literally. The crime fighter
was already seriously diminished from a fight with four
club-wielding thugs when Ramoto advanced, twirling a
pair of the pearl-handled slice-and-dice instruments that
gave him his nickname. When he regained consciousness,
he could not explain what happened. One second he was

slashing at his foe, then everything went black. The police evidence team bagged the matched pair of straightedge razors, noting that they were as pristine as when first manufactured. One rookie shook his head in amazement, but his more-seasoned partner took it in stride.

"It don't matter what the bad guys bring to the party," he told the rookie, "they all got to dance to the Batman's tune."

After a short stint in the steam room, Bruce Wayne showered and shaved. He dressed rapidly, then descended to the living room where he found Alfred engrossed before the giant-screen TV. The image was Hellgate Prison, an overhead shot from the network helicopter. Bruce took a seat next to his old friend, raising his eyebrows in a question. Alfred responded by patting the air in front of him in a clear "Wait a minute" gesture.

The TV image shifted to a close-up of a stocky black man dressed in a dark blue suit. The knot of his red silk tie was pulled loose, and his white shirt was rumpled. His appearance was that of a man accustomed to command— under stress but remaining in control.

As the camera pulled back, the viewer could see that the black man was surrounded by a horseshoe-shaped crowd of reporters, some brandishing microphones, others with pencils poised over pads.

"One at a time, damn it!" the black man shouted. "We stopped a potential riot inside—I sure don't need one out here! You first, all right?" he asked, pointing at a middle-aged Latino whose beautifully cut gray suit somehow matched his gunfighter's eyes.

"Warden Richardson, is it true that an escape tunnel was discovered under Hellgate Prison?"

"Yes, Mr. Gonzales, that's *exactly* what we discovered. Next!"

"How close was the tunnel to completion?" an Oriental woman wearing a headset asked, thrusting a microphone forward, her clear voice neatly slicing through the din.

"If you mean distance, I'd estimate about another twenty, thirty feet, Ms. Hong," the warden replied. "If you're asking about time, maybe another month. Six weeks at the outside."

"How was it discovered?" asked a granite-faced man whose press pass protruded from the battered fedora on his head, 1950s style.

"Mr. Hechler, I don't know why it is, but every question you ask keeps taking me to the same answer."

"Which is?" the reporter challenged.

"The information is confidential. To reveal it would be to—"

"—compromise the integrity of an ongoing investigation," the reporter finished for the warden, sarcasm dripping from his tongue.

"Next!" the warden snapped.

"Is it true about the body—?" a blonde woman in a red miniskirt started to ask.

"Look, give me a break here," the warden bellowed. "I'm going to tell you everything I am authorized to release. I'm going to tell you *once*, understand? Now listen up: at approximately oh-six-hundred hours earlier this morning, we received a tip from an anonymous source of past-proven reliability. Acting on the information we received, we waited until first light and then began a search for an escape tunnel. At approximately eleven-fifteen, the tunnel was discovered. No inmates were apprehended in the process of working on the tunnel. However, at a spot fairly near to the tunnel entrance, we did find the body of one Lester Tuxley, a recently admitted inmate. Tuxley had been stabbed to death. Whoever did it knew his work—the stabbing had all the earmarks of a professional assassination. The weapon was a shank, apparently fashioned in the prison machine shop. No fingerprints were found on the weapon. As of now, we have no suspects.''

"Did Tuxley have any known enemies?'' one reporter shouted.

"I'm sure he did,'' the warden replied gravely. "He was a child molester, a chronic recidivist with over eighty victims to his everlasting disgrace.''

"I mean, did he have any enemies *inside* the prison?'' the same reporter asked.

"There's all kinds of reasons to end up in a place like this,'' the warden said, glaring in the direction of his questioner. "A . . . person like Tuxley . . . well, anything's possible.'' To the veterans among the reporters, the warden's shrug was more eloquent than his words.

The TV image of the area outside Hellgate Prison was replaced by an elaborately coifed anchorman inside the studio. "You've heard the latest, live from the scene. We will return periodically as new information develops. In the meantime, from the world of sports, we have . . .''

Alfred hit the Mute button on the remote control. "A rather unexpected development, isn't it, Master Bruce?''

Bruce closed his eyes, the better to recapture the previous night's encounter with the Middleman. He could still see the look in the master criminal's eyes, could still feel the heat of his palm right through the glass. And he remembered the Middleman warning him that if he used Lester Tuxley as an introduction to the world of child molestation profiteers, he would have to say the encounter took place before today.

"Maybe not," was all Bruce said.

Not another word was exchanged between the two men for several hours. Then, as night descended on Wayne Manor, its owner descended to the Batcave. Alfred watched him go, his noble face expressionless.

More hours passed.

In his private suite of rooms, Alfred sat before a magnificent zebrawood desk, running his left hand gently over the inlaid top of black-veined dark green marble as his right hand cradled his jaw. His deep-set hazel eyes had that particular glaze produced by focus on the middle distance. With the exception of the gentle rhythmic movements of his left hand, to an observer he might have been cast in stone.

In the Batcave, a man caught between states of being sat in the same position. The man wore the Batman's costume, but with the cowl retracted so that his head was bare. The final stage in the transformation from dilettante to vigilante—the specially designed gloves, of titanium mesh laced inside fireproof fabric—lay untouched on the clear Lexan surface of the utility table. The man's normally blue eyes were fixed in the same middle-distance stare as Alfred's, but this halfway-man's eyes were obsidian . . . reflecting all, revealing nothing but that reflection.

Hours passed.

Alfred came out of his trancelike state with a sudden snap of his eyes. He appeared exhausted but resolute—a man who had wrestled his conscience to an honorable draw—a man who found, as all truth seekers do, that he must be his own standard of honor.

"A man must stand," he said softly to himself, remembering his father's words to him many decades ago. Remembering the credo by which his father had lived. "Be he the first to stand or the last, a man must stand," the father had told his adoring son. "And if there is only one man, then that man must stand alone."

Alfred stood up. He walked stiffly to where a cherrywood bookcase had been built into the wall. He grasped one of the lower shelves and thrust upward with all his strength. For a long five seconds, nothing happened. Then, gradually, an empty section of the bookshelf rotated, revealing an extraordinary example of the cabinetmaker's art—a cribbage board of such intricate design that it appeared to have been fashioned by magicians. The board was actually a box, hinged so that the playing pegs could be carried within it. What at first glance seemed to be gleaming bone-white wood with a slight yellowish cast was, in reality, hand-carved ivory. Each of the long series of parallel holes designed to hold the playing pegs was lined with a tiny ring of gold, each hand-set to microscopic tolerances.

Alfred opened the hinged box and extracted a handful of playing pegs. Like the board itself, the pegs were ivory. Each was tipped with a perfect dot of color—half were red, half were green. Rubies and emeralds, Alfred knew, each faceted so minutely that only a *sense* of color was experienced by the onlooker—the actual microgems could not be seen with the naked eye.

From inside a never-used liquor cabinet, Alfred took a velvet pad of royal purple. He laid the pad on the desktop, then placed the cribbage board on it. He then began to insert the playing pegs in what seemed a haphazard pattern, his hands moving with the confidence of a neurosurgeon. The process took several minutes. Alfred bent over the board, checking the red and green dots of sparkling light, occasionally moving one of the playing pegs over a notch.

Finally Alfred nodded as though confirming a long-held suspicion and inserted one more peg. As soon as the tiny peg locked in, a thin tray popped out of one end of the board. Inside the tray was a key.

Alfred plucked the key from the tray and strode confidently to his bedroom. There, he went to the head of a double bed. He pulled sharply on the left bedpost. The post broke at right angles, hinged in such a way that it was invisible to anything less than a microscope's inspection. Alfred looked at the lower part of the bedpost, located a keyhole with his fingertips, and inserted the key. As he turned the key, he pulled upward, extracting a long metal cylinder. After restoring the bedpost to its original position, Alfred returned to his study. There, he opened the cylinder slowly and respectfully, his manner suggesting some sort of religious ceremony.

A tightly rolled tube of papers emerged. Alfred carefully smoothed them flat on the desktop, anchoring each corner with a brass paperweight. He then opened what appeared to be a slim attaché case of black anodized aluminum. Inside, the case was lined with cork encased in foam rubber—in each corner, a slight overlap allowed for documents to be held in place. Alfred inserted the papers facedown, one at a time, checking each sheet for precision alignment. Once satisfied, he inserted a connector plug into a porthole on the side of the case. A wire ran from the plug into a transformer, which was itself plugged into a wall socket. Alfred pressed a button on the transformer, and a faint humming sound filled the room.

Alfred watched unconcerned as tiny wisps of fog exited from a series of pores in the case—he knew humidity was a necessary part of the restoration process. The original papers had not been of archival quality, and Alfred had been unwilling to trust their structural integrity to photocopying. The specially designed preservation-restoration box was one of a kind. Although it resembled other similar units used by professional document transporters—hence the attaché case appearance—the use of precious metals and near-zero tolerances made the cost of this particular unit far too expensive for such pedestrian purposes.

Alfred had religiously performed the preservation-restoration ritual many times over the years. Each time, when the unit had done its work, he had returned the papers to their hiding place.

But this time, Alfred stood holding the newly rejuvenated papers in his two hands for several minutes.

Then the man for whom loyalty was life left the room.

Even in that psychoemotional borderland between alternate states of consciousness, the Batman possessed a sense of his surroundings so delicate that it could detect the slightest molecular shifts in the empty air—a motion sensor so refined it exceeded the abilities of any device known to science. Even seated at his desk with his back to the elevator entrance to the Batcave, he could feel the presence of another. Yet his psyche was unalarmed—it could only be Alfred.

With an effort of will, the Batman turned his head, watching his old friend—his oldest friend—approach. Unable to speak, the unmasked face raised an eyebrow, asking "Why?"

Not, "Why are *you* here?" but "Why am *I*?"

Alfred had been nonverbally asked that same question many times over the years. In the past, he had been content to pat the Batman on the shoulder and assure him that, someday, all would be known to him. Such a gesture was not the hollow placation of an uninvolved parent dealing with a questioning child—it was a sacred promise from a friend who knew the truth. A true friend who would, someday, share that truth.

"It is time," is all Alfred said.

The Batman's eyes snapped into life, the obsidian glaze instantly replaced by eyes of glowing cobalt. "How

should I—?'' the seated man asked, one hand on the
Batman mask, the other hovering near the Velcro closure
to the crime fighter's costume.

"Stay as you are," Alfred replied, endorsing neither
the Batman nor the Bruce Wayne persona. "This is for
all of you."

The Batman came to his feet, the movement tentative,
uncertain. He followed Alfred to a section of the Batcave
that he had never entered alone. That small section had
been set aside for those times when Alfred had to serve
as the Batman's midmission communications-and-infor-
mation link, sometimes for days at a time.

In startling incongruity to the ultramodern look of
the Batcave, Alfred's section was a throwback to the last
century. A pair of comfortable old oxblood leather easy
chairs sat on a hand-hooked rug of muted red and gold,
standing as twin sentinels before the grate of a white marble fireplace. An old-fashioned floor lamp with a Tiffany
shade sat next to one of the chairs—the other chair had
a matching leather ottoman. Clearly, one chair was for
reading, the other for Alfred to catch a quick nap while
awaiting the next contact from the Batman. As if to confirm
that status, the ottoman was covered with a neatly folded
afghan of dark blue wool.

Following Alfred's wordless gesture, the Batman took
the chair with the reading lamp. Alfred approached, waiting patiently until the seated figure met his eyes.

"I know you are in pain," Alfred said. "It is time you
know the cause . . . the *root* cause. Depression is no stranger
to you, I know. And I know how these . . . forays into child
abuse investigation have troubled you so deeply. It has
all come together, as I knew it someday would. It is all
connected, and you are the center." Without another

word, he handed a thick sheaf of papers to the seated man.

"What is—?"

"An investigator's journal," Alfred replied.

"I can see that," the seated figure said, his eyes flicking over the tiny, precise handwriting. "But whose is it?"

"Your mother's," Alfred said, his voice grave. "It is time you knew . . . not just what she did, but what she was."

"I . . ."

"Read it," Alfred interrupted gently. "Read it all. I'll be right here. When you're finished, I will answer any questions that you have."

Hour after hour slipped by. If the seated figure was aware of this, he gave no sign. Alfred occasionally arose from his own chair, sometimes to work the kinks out of his legs, sometimes to bring a glass of water to the seated figure. The Batman sipped from the water glass unconsciously, not aware he was doing so, as totally absorbed in the papers before him as a heat-seeking missile locked onto its target.

The seated figure's breathing dropped into precombat mode—slow, measured, and deep. He read as though each word were a multifaceted diamond, holding them up to the light one at a time, observing the refraction, the color, the depth . . . squeezing every drop from the precious link to his mother—a link that spanned the chasm between Then and Now.

Tiny alterations in his neuromuscular systems produced in the Batman the same effect a normal person would get from eight hours' refreshing sleep. He read and reread the pages, careful to keep them in their original order, as they were not numbered. He rubbed a corner of the paper between his fingertips, feeling the texture of his mother's life in the fibers.

Outside the Batcave, time unfolded. Day gave way to night as the calendar inched forward. But inside, time advanced and retreated in instantaneous jolts as the seated figure mentally connected his mother's life to his own, moving between them with the speed of thought.

Finally the seated figure put the pages down. His facial features relaxed. His eyes closed.

Alfred watched the sleep-trance. Watched as he had watched the boy, the teenager, and the man. Watched with the patience that had allowed him to wait almost thirty years for this single moment.

It is never truth that determines the course of history, Alfred mused to himself—it was the *effect* of truth on those who acted and, in turn, they upon it.

In another few hours, he would have the answer.

When the seated figure opened his eyes, Alfred was waiting. "Can I—?"

"I'm all right, Alfred. The information was just . . . too much. It overamped my circuits, that's all."

"I understand, Master Bruce."

"Do you, my old friend? Can you tell me, then? Is it all true?"

"Without question."

"My mother . . . my mother was an investigative sociologist?"

"She was."

"Have you read . . . ?" he asked, indicating the papers now resting on an end table under the lamp.

"No," Alfred replied. "I have not."

"Yet you know what they contain?"

"Some of it. That was not the point, however. Your mother entrusted me with her journals. And with that trust came a pledge—a pledge of honor. I was to place the journals in your hands. In your hands and no one else's, no matter what."

"But when—?"

"The timing was to be my choice," Alfred said. "If your mother . . . lived, she would make that choice. If she did not, it was up to me."

"Not to my father?" Bruce Wayne asked.

"No," Alfred replied simply, his tone of voice brooking no discussion.

"Did you know what she was . . . investigating when she . . . died?"

"Yes. I knew it quite well. It was the single topic that consumed your mother for many years."

"My mother . . . all these years I had no *sense* of her. Just . . . memories. Baking cookies, reading me stories. I thought she was a . . . housewife."

"She *was* a housewife, Master Bruce. But that was never *all* she was."

"Alfred, these journals . . . they seem unbelievable to me. My mother was investigating an international ring of pedophiles. These organizational charts, look . . ." he said, thrusting some of the papers across to Alfred. "It was a perfect pyramid, a typical organized crime monolith. See here," he said, reaching over to point his index finger at a meticulously drawn flowchart. "This is how they produced the child pornography. My mother traced it all up from the roots—the procurers, the photographers, the developers, the printers, the distributors . . . everything! She used the classic 'follow the dollars' investigative technique."

"That technique was hardly 'classic' when your mother used it," Alfred said. "In fact, I believe the technique is one of your mother's great contributions to the investigative profession."

"I . . . never knew."

"Your mother did not *want* you to know, Master Bruce. She was in a situation of great personal danger. The targets of her investigation would stop at nothing to neutralize her. In fact, her disguise was similar to your own. As the public thinks of Bruce Wayne as a playboy, the same public thought of your mother as, as you put it, a housewife."

"But didn't my father—?"

"You have read the newspaper accounts of their murder many times, Master Bruce. How were your parents described?"

"As Dr. and Mrs. Thomas Wayne . . . Yes! I understand what you mean now. It was as though she had a life only as a wife. I suppose that was common back when I was born. But these papers . . . what she was doing . . . it seems so . . ."

"Dangerous?"

"Yes," the seated figure said. "Very dangerous."

"Your mother knew the dangers, Master Bruce. She was a woman of great courage. And she would not be deterred from her mission."

"But if she knew who was responsible . . . ?"

"She knew *some* of the people," Alfred told him. "Your mother was the first to understand the organizational capabilities of child molesters and others who prey upon children. The world viewed such despicable creatures as isolated aberrations. Your mother was the first to link child molestation with organized crime."

"You mean like narcotics? Or loan-sharking? Labor racketeering?"

"No, Master Bruce. The pedophile syndicates were more concerned with their personal . . . pleasures," Alfred said, his lips involuntarily curling at the idea. "It apparently took quite a few of . . . them to manufacture and distribute their filth."

"How did she—?"

"She did it all," Alfred interrupted. "She interviewed the child victims, she placed ads in the underground news-letters, she made undercover purchases, she paid some of the offenders for their information. She had a network of her own. A network of like-minded people around the world. Just as the pedophiles had constructed their net-works, your mother and her colleagues were tracking them."

"Where would she find the . . . victims?" the seated man asked. "I thought all the child abuse records were confidential."

"Master Bruce, at the time your mother was doing her investigations, there *was* no Child Abuse Registry. The more egregious cases were referred to the police."

"And the rest were—?"

"Ignored," Alfred said flatly. "People your age take things like a Child Abuse Hotline for granted. But if it wasn't for courageous people like your mother, those things wouldn't exist."

"I . . . understand. But I still don't see where she could find child abuse victims to interview. How could she—?"

"Your mother always said that if you wanted to inter-view victims of child abuse, all you had to do was drive up to Belladonna Farms."

"The institution for juvenile delinquents? But . . ."

"Master Bruce, all you have before you are your mother's investigative journals. Those are field notes, not operational theory. Your mother's thesis was that there is no biogenetic code for criminality. She always maintained that you cannot control *who* you are, but you have the ultimate decision-making power over *what* you are."

"I'm not certain that—"

"Behavior is the truth," Alfred cut in. "The ultimate truth. You are what you *do*. Children are born with different genetic allotments, from the color of their eyes to their intellectual capacity, but the rest is what they themselves contribute. The worst thing about the abuse of children is that it robs the victims of some of that capacity. Your mother also said that today's victim could be tomorrow's predator unless we intervene properly. She was talking about children, Master Bruce."

"So my mother was a . . ."

"Crime fighter," Alfred finished for him. "A crime fighter with a secret identity."

Silence descended over his last words. A heavy, ink-black silence darker than any midnight. The seated figure slumped. The sound of quiet sobbing entered the silence. The sobbing of a child—a child robbed of his childhood.

Alfred rose to his feet. He placed one hand on the shoulder of the man he had devoted his life to protect. And, once again, he waited.

It was a long time before the child stopped crying. But when he did, it was a fully focused adult who took his place. The seated figure surged to his feet, oblivious to the contrast between the Batman costume and Bruce Wayne's blandly handsome face. He stalked over to the giant computer, his mouth set in a straight line. He ran page after page of his mother's journal through an optical disc scanner, watching as each page was converted to computer-readable type and simultaneously pulled into one of the huge machine's ninety-gigabyte parallel hard drives. Then he rapidly typed a series of commands:

> **Martha Wayne Journal // Pull names, all**
> **Sort**
> **Search**
> *Against?*
> **ALL RECORDS**

One by one, the computer searched/sorted/matched each of the names mentioned in Martha Wayne's investigative journals. Without exception, all **LOCATE** inquiries ended on variations of the same note:

> *Deceased, Homicide, Gunshot*
> *Missing, Presumed Dead*
> *Deceased, Suicide, Suspicious Circumstances*
> *Deceased, Vehicular Accident*
> *Deceased, Natural Causes*
> *Deceased, Blunt Instrument*
> *Deceased, Prostate Cancer*
> *Whereabouts Unknown, Last Information Indicates Residence in Udon Khai*
> **Locate / Udon Khai**
> *Southeast Asia*
> **Principal Industry / Udon Khai**
> *No age of consent for sexual intercourse*

What kind of "industry" was that? His face a study in puzzlement, the man seated at the console typed the same question, changing the wording slightly in the hope that the computer could clarify its cryptic statement.

What industry Udon Khai?

Sex

Open / sex

Sex with children

Other industries?

Related: Transportation, procurement, souvenirs

Define Last

Sex with children, photographed to customer's specifications

The seated figure ran both hands through his thick black hair. Then he took a deep yoga breath, drawing the air down past his chest all the way to his groin. As he exhaled, he compressed his abdominal muscles, clearing his thoughts.

Summary, all names

N=77

Deceased=71

Missing, Presumed Dead=3

Whereabouts Unknown=2

Whereabouts Known=1

Only three of them maybe still alive. Only one of them for sure. All that work. All that exhaustive investigation. And now, what was . . . ?

A sudden thought invaded, insistent and intrusive, demanding attention. "Alfred," the man seated at the console asked quietly, never doubting for a moment that his old friend would be in the room, somewhere behind him, "the computer doesn't cross-connect any of these names to organized crime, even the one old man who is allegedly still alive. Do you think any of them knew?"

"Knew what, Master Bruce?"

"What my mother was doing. That she was on their trail?"

"Oh, yes," Alfred said, a thin vein of sorrow in his voice. "They knew quite well."

"Then . . ." The crime fighter turned back to the computer and slowly typed: **Case # 1**. The computer screen instantly popped into life with all the information known about the killer who had gunned down his parents right before a child's terrorized eyes.

The computer display was unnecessary—the horror was indelibly etched into the memory of the child Bruce Wayne:

M\X-AR {Mother: Martha Wayne} Deceased, Homicide incident to Armed Robbery.

F\X-AR {Father: Thomas Wayne, MD} Deceased, Homicide incident to Armed Robbery.

W=HG {Murder Weapon: Handgun} never recovered

WMM\/UNK/UNK\–35 68–71″\SMT=UNK//UNS {Perpetrator Description} First Broadcast.

APP\NW\D-RA {Perpetrator} Apprehended, No Warrant, Deceased, Resisting Arrest.

GW/7/9mm\NrA? {Autopsy} Gunshot wounds, 7 hits, 9mm, Suspect Nonregulation Ammunition, Not Resolved.

JOE NMI CHILL {Name}

The computer screen provided nothing new. Nothing that the Batman had not long since memorized by heart— the permanently traumatized heart of a child whose parents vanished in the split second it takes a bullet to do its homicidal work.

"My . . . mother . . ." The Batman's head throbbed with pain as he fought for self-control. "Follow it down!" he commanded himself, his fingers flying over the keyboard.

Connect Known Associates

None

The seated figure nodded. How many times had he asked the same question? Too many to count. He sat there, immobile, as though he were a computer himself, awaiting human command to come into life.

"Go on, Master Bruce," Alfred said, his hand still on his charge's shoulder.

The Batman extended his hands, watched carefully until all trace of tremor was gone, then typed a new message to the computer.

Inquiries: Case # 1?

N=88

Breakdown by Category?

GPD=77, NM=31

No big surprise, the Batman thought to himself. Seventy-seven inquiries from the Gotham Police Department, another thirty-one from the news media. Dr. and Mrs. Thomas Wayne had been one of the most socially prominent couples in Gotham—their deaths not only spurred a massive law enforcement effort, it was front-page news. How could . . . ?

Had the Batman been watching the computer's digital clock, he would have noticed a passage of more than an hour. An hour in which he hunted in his mind. Then:

Inquiries outside assignment // Media?

N=0

Inquiries outside assignment // Police?

N=1

Identify

Lieutenant Alexander Horton, GPD, Commander, Sex Crimes Unit

"Why would the head of the Sex Crimes Unit be asking about the hunt for my parents' murderer?" the Batman asked. "Besides, he . . . Alfred! He was the one who—"

"It could be for any number of reasons," Alfred interrupted smoothly. "Just go on . . . finish it."

The Batman's posture changed. His fingers drilled the keyboard, his eyes magneted to the screen.

Connect: Lieutenant Alexander Horton, Gotham Police Department

To?

Martha Wayne Journal, Investigative Targets

Searching. Please wait . . .

The two men watched as the computer graphically displayed the complicated charts hand drawn by Martha Wayne so many years ago. Watched as names swapped in and out of various boxes, watched the arrows of the flowcharts.

And waited.

Then . . .

Lieutenant Alexander Horton: Verified meetings with Barbara Jane Slocum, N=7

Both men's eyes riveted on the screen. They had each been shocked to see a woman's name on the list of pedophiles being investigated—seeing it again so soon ignited a recognition flash.

Barbara Jane Slocum: Category?

Deceased, Suicide

Open / Suicide

The Batman's eyes skimmed the screen as information scrolled past. *Place Found, Contents of Note, Autopsy, Occupation* . . . the list of data was endless. None of it appeared to be of value, but suddenly, popping up as smooth and deadly as a moray eel:

Investigating officer: Lieutenant Alexander Horton

Ignoring Alfred's involuntary gasp from somewhere behind his shoulder, the Batman typed:

Bank Records // Barbara Jane Slocum

Within seconds, the computer told a truth that had been hidden from human eyes for decades. Currency transfers from a bank in Udon Khai to Barbara Jane Slocum ranging from twenty-five to one hundred thousand dollars, each transfer preceding a meeting between her and Lieutenant Horton.

"How brazen," Alfred muttered.

"Not so much," the Batman replied. "All the transfers were done in the precomputer age. And before banks had to report currency transactions of ten thousand or more like they have to do now."

"Perhaps the IRS, Master Wayne?"

"Right," the Batman said, his attention turning back to the keyboard.

For Barbara Jane Slocum, all the transactions had been reported—not as income, but as gifts from her uncle, one William X. Malady.

William X. Malady.

The one person the computer identified as still alive.

Alive and living in Udon Khai.

As far as he had ever reported to the IRS, Lieutenant Horton's income had never exceeded his police paycheck.

From there on, the trail markers were unmistakable. Horton had purchased a number of expensive toys for himself years ago. A Cadillac Eldorado Biarritz convertible, a forty-foot cabin cruiser, a condo on the ninth hole of a golf course in Florida. And his gambling losses averaged more per year than his entire police salary.

Within weeks after each currency transfer to Slocum, some significant event had been recorded in Martha Wayne's journals. A raid on a kiddie porn factory that had been planned for months failed—the inhabitants had cleared out the night before. A witness prepared to testify against a pedophile ring had been thrown from the roof of a government building in downtown Gotham. Suitcases full of evidence against a child prostitution syndicate had disappeared from the Police Evidence Locker.

The last currency transfer—and the biggest—had been two weeks before an event that tipped the balance in favor of the child sex merchants, an event that had never been connected to the secret war raging in the underground.

The killing of Martha Wayne.

The computer screen's paper-white glow filled the Batcave, but the man who sat before it saw only a red haze.

Three hours later, Bruce Wayne and Alfred sat across from each other in the sunken living room of Wayne Manor. Suddenly Bruce got to his feet and began pacing.

"All my life, Alfred. All my life, I have wondered *why*. Why my parents were killed, why such horrors exist. In honor of my parents, I devoted my life to fighting crime. But you know what? I haven't been fighting *crime*, old friend—I've been fighting *criminals*. And now I know, they're not the same.

"I'm not 'Bruce Wayne,' whoever *that* is. That's not

me. For so long, I've wondered why I come alive only as the Batman. Alfred, now I know. Bruce Wayne is a hollow man. A convenient disguise, that's all. The Batman is a warrior."

The pacing man suddenly halted, spinning back on one heel and bringing both arms down to trail across his path—a martial arts blocking maneuver beyond the comprehension of Bruce Wayne. The man faced his old friend squarely, his voice deepening with conviction: "I am a warrior. From a warrior descended. My mother gave birth to Bruce Wayne, but her work . . . her *life* gave birth to Batman. Her death only speeded the process."

"Master Bruce, I—"

"The criminal underworld has always feared me," the Batman interrupted. "For good reason, perhaps. From this moment on, what they need to fear is my mother . . . the completion of my mother's work."

Alfred nodded gravely, his eyes heavy with truth. "I knew this would be so," he said. "Your mother knew you would have her journals someday. And somehow, she knew the effect they would have on you. That is why I waited as long as I did."

"You did right," the Batman assured Alfred. "But now, I—"

"Master Bruce, please wait. There is one more thing I must give you. A message from your mother." Without another word, he left the room. When he returned, a parchment scroll tied with a black ribbon was in his hand. He presented it to Bruce with the gracious formality that was his hallmark.

The Batman carefully removed the ribbon and opened the scroll. At the top of the page was a short series of pictographic characters. Underneath were a few words in English. "What is this?" he asked.

"It is a haiku, Master Bruce," Alfred told him. "At the top is the original Japanese, below it is the translation. It was your mother's wish that you have this before you walked the path she had marked for you."

Bruce Wayne looked at the parchment. But it was the Batman who listened:

Warrior, heed this
when you battle with demons
aim not at their hearts

That evening, Debra Kane trudged through the refuse scattered throughout an alley in the misery-splattered neighborhood known as the Bowery. She good-naturedly bemoaned her high heels, feeling much more comfortable in sneakers and jeans. But her job required a professional appearance. "Even if it doesn't provide professional paychecks," she thought to herself.

Her car was parked at the end of the alley, right next to a huge green Dumpster. It wasn't exactly an ideal spot, but the City Council had not seen fit to issue Privileged Parking stickers to Child Protective caseworkers, obviously believing such largess was better bestowed on doctors who never made house calls and major campaign contributors who did.

Debra's high heels clicked against the alley's cobblestones. As she was reaching into her purse for the car keys, she suddenly heard another set of footsteps close behind her. She whirled to confront whoever was following her, car keys protruding through her closed fist. The man pulled up short, hands in the air.

"Don't shoot," he chuckled.

"What do you want?" Debra Kane asked, not a trace of fear in her voice.

"Why, sweetheart, I don't want much. Just . . . *you*, if you get my drift."

"Come on, then!" Debra challenged him, turning sideways, offering her opponent only a profile, shifting her weight to her back foot so she could push off powerfully when he attacked.

"Take it easy, sweetheart," the man said. "No use rushing things. How about if you just—"

The man's voice died in his throat as the Batman stepped forward from the shadows. "Your partner is going to be late for your meeting," the night-rider said to him, his voice perfectly matching the dry ice of his eyes.

The man who had been stalking Debra Kane whipped a length of bicycle chain from around his waist. With an explosion of breath to add strength to his thrust, he charged the Batman, swinging the chain with practiced skill. But the Batman flowed beneath the swinging chain as smoothly as water under a bridge. He came out of his crouch with an explosive side kick, driving the would-be rapist into the alley wall with sufficient force to raise a small cloud of brick dust. The man crumpled to the ground, the chain falling from his fingers.

Debra Kane stood transfixed. Like every other resident of Gotham, she had heard the rumors of the Legend Who Lives, as the Batman was called in the Oriental community. But hearing was not the same as experiencing. He didn't seem like a man at all—more like a powerful shadow . . . a *force* beyond the understanding of mere humans.

"Thank you," she said simply. "But I could have—"

"I don't think so," the Batman interrupted politely. "If you look behind your car, you'll see this one's partner. The idea was to have you concentrate on him while his partner took you out from behind."

"Is he—?"

"He won't be doing anything for a while," the Batman assured her. "And with some great difficulty for some time to come. Please wait here."

The crime fighter walked past Debra to where her car had been parked at the end of the alley. When he returned, a human figure was draped over his shoulder. Moving as though the man on his shoulder were weightless, the Batman dropped him unceremoniously on the ground next to his partner. A few seconds' work with the specialized restraints of his own invention and the two were immobilized. Even in the highly unlikely event that the two thugs regained consciousness before the police arrived, they wouldn't be going anywhere.

The Batman activated his wrist communicator to open the private channel between him and the commissioner's office. "Two attempted rapists, down and restrained, near the mouth of the alley between Forty-eighth and Forty-ninth. If they fail to confess, contact Ms. Debra Kane, Gotham CPS. Ms. Kane was the intended victim. One of them made a direct attempt, and can be ID'ed by Ms. Kane. The other was lurking behind her official vehicle. The vehicle has been disabled—you will find an ice pick in the right rear tire—it should have the lurker's fingerprints all over the handle. The vehicle will remain in place so that your forensics people can gather the evidence.''

The Batman closed the frequency before he could be questioned, his eyes on Debra Kane.

"How will I—?''

"I would be honored to escort you out of here,'' the night-rider said.

As Debra Kane and the Batman emerged from the mouth of the alley, the caseworker said, "It's quite a distance from here to my apartment. Too far to walk in these heels. And I can't see a cab stopping for . . . you. I can just—''

"That won't be necessary,'' the Batman replied, touching a transmitter on his utility belt. "I'm sure if we just wait here, we'll have transportation in a minute.''

Debra Kane opened her mouth to reply, but before a word could pass her lips, a vehicle slipped silently around the corner and came to a stop before them. Too long and massive to be a motor vehicle, the dark shape reminded Debra of the famous ICE train. She had ridden it last summer from Hamburg to Frankfurt while on the vacation it had taken her nearly six years to save for on her meager salary.

The Batman touched his utility belt again. The Batmobile's canopy slid back with a faint hydraulic hiss, revealing a cigar-shaped interior. Behind the driver's compartment was a pair of passenger seats, each one equipped with a five-point racing harness instead of a conventional seat belt.

Debra Kane viewed the sight dubiously. The passenger

seat looked comfortable enough, but there was no door to the vehicle. She gamely hiked up her skirt and tried to throw one leg over the sill, but she couldn't shift her weight sufficiently and staggered backward. Before she could react, she found herself off the ground . . . in the arms of the Batman.

"With your permission . . ." the masked man said politely.

Debra Kane didn't have time to reply before she was gently lowered into the passenger seat.

"Fasten your belts," the Batman said, just before he vaulted into the driver's compartment. The crime fighter's fingers flew over the array of buttons in the overhead console. The Batmobile's shielding immediately slid into place. A quick systems-check indicated no problems. The Batman shoved a stubby floor-mounted lever forward, and the Batmobile crept away from the curb.

Unlike the conventional driveshaft of a modern motor vehicle, the Batmobile transferred power from the turbines to all four wheels through a series of massive iridium screws. The unique machine had no "gears" as such— adjustments were made by varying the number and intensity of the screws called into play.

For city cruising, the Batman used only the small auxiliary turbines mounted just behind the rear wheels. Each of the auxiliary exhausts was the diameter of a coffee can lid—huge by automotive standards, but dwarfed by the main turbine, which was set much higher and centered in the Batmobile's rear deck.

"Don't be intimidated," Debra Kane counseled herself. "So what if you don't ride in a Batmobile every day— don't just sit there with your mouth open like a little girl on the Ferris wheel." She leaned forward as far as the safety harness allowed, watching the passing scenes over the Batman's shoulder through the observation slit that ran ninety degrees from the midpoint on each side. "How can you see what's behind you?" she asked, noting with pride the calmness of her own voice.

"The minicams do that," the Batman replied, tapping the row of video screens mounted in a wide strip across the top of the overhead console.

"Can people see in?"

"No. The observation slit is one-way Lexan."

"Lexan? Is that—?"

"Bulletproof," the crime fighter finished for her. "The entire vehicle is designed to withstand anything from small-arms fire right up to bombs and missiles."

"In Gotham?" Debra Kane asked.

"Heavy weapons are easy to obtain in America," he replied. "*Too* easy. We have sufficient technology to ward off virtually any explosive, but the trade-off in agility wouldn't be worth it."

"Agility?" Debra laughed. "This thing is bigger than a Greyhound bus."

"It's a bit deceptive," the crime fighter said quietly. "There's more to it than meets the eye."

"And not just the car," Debra thought to herself, leaning back in her seat and watching the streets, trying to gauge the vehicle's speed.

Debra quickly realized that a valid estimate of speed was impossible—the sensation was more akin to flying than driving. The Batmobile's on-board computer independently balanced each wheel gyroscopically. The computer also controlled the height of the undercarriage, rising for the potholed city streets, lowering for maximum aerodynamics when in pursuit mode. The Batmobile also featured a complete ground-effects system that could exert a vacuum force, increasing adhesion beyond that of any race car. Debra tried to estimate speed by watching other cars on the road, but the Batmobile flicked past them so smoothly that only a *sensation* of passage could be felt.

The Batmobile worked its way through the rabbit's warren of dark streets that the newspapers called Crime Alley. Because so many of its residents were transients, the neighborhood was devoid of political clout. As a result, the overpopulated and underpoliced area had become a toxic waste dump for "businesses" not wanted in other areas. From topless bars to triple-X movies, from narcotics to firearms, Crime Alley was a one-stop shopping center, catering to anyone with money to spend.

Debra Kane sat silently, not questioning that, somehow, the mystical masked man who sat close enough for her to touch knew her studio apartment was just on the other side of Crime Alley. Suddenly the Batmobile slipped into a side street and came to a stop.

"What's wrong?" Debra asked.

"I'm not sure," the Batman replied. "Let's see what the probes say."

Debra watched in fascination as the video monitor next to the Batman came to life with the characteristic green-and-white glow indicating light-gathering technology at work. As the Batman maneuvered the probes, the video image stabilized to show half a dozen men lounging outside a bar, blocking the narrow sidewalk, forcing passersby into the street. Although the image was soundless, Debra's practiced eye recognized the group for what it was—one of the numerous crews of opportunistic street criminals that inhabited Crime Alley. Small-time in the extreme, they subsisted on a combination of welfare fraud, illegal food stamps, and petty theft. Most were alcoholics—all were bullies. Marginal human beings, as anonymous in Crime Alley as alligators in the Everglades. But unlike alligators, occasionally the bullies would attack for the pure perverse pleasure of it.

"I don't see—"

"Watch . . ." the Batman interrupted.

A woman came into view in the extreme right corner of the video monitor—a woman with long red hair and a spectacular shape that was glaringly obvious in the micro-mini and fishnet stockings she wore. Above the tiny skirt, the woman wore a short-sleeved striped jersey several sizes too small. Her spike heels were so high she was forced to walk in a careful, mincing manner that only added to the general jiggle. As the woman approached, the crew's posture changed, switching in a heartbeat from idler to predator.

From the opposite side approached another typical target of the bullies—a man in a wheelchair, his lap covered by a blanket even in the heat of the summer night. Two of the bullies looked in his direction, but immediately decided the woman was better prey.

As Debra Kane watched the video, the Batman's right hand flashed, throwing the Batmobile into gear. The huge vehicle roared out of the alley's mouth on full turbine, eating up the ground to the videoed scene. The Batmobile took corner after corner as smoothly as a jungle cat, finally hitting the street where the bullies waited for the woman.

"Stay here!" the Batman snapped over his shoulder at Debra Kane, simultaneously slamming his fist down on a large red button marked SQ3. The canopy instantly retracted as the Batman launched into the air, propelled by the twin air cannons built into the driver's seat. Debra's jaw dropped in amazement as the canopy slammed shut just over her head. She stared at the video screen, utterly transfixed.

The Batman's launch became a perfect parabola—one full midair twist and he landed lightly on his feet, dropping precisely between the man in the wheelchair and the bullies who were still facing the approaching woman. Suddenly the blanket dropped from the lap of the man in the wheelchair, revealing a sawed-off double-barreled shotgun. The man in the wheelchair was cobra-quick, but the Batman moved with the speed of a turbo-charged mongoose, kicking the weapon out of the seated man's hands. He whirled, just in time to duck under a shot fired in his direction . . . not by the gang of bullies but by the redheaded woman!

The Batman lanced through the bullies, knocking them aside as though they were department store dummies, a Batarang poised in his right hand. By the time he had a clear sight line to the woman, she had kicked off her spike heels and was standing in a combat-shooting crouch, a submachine gun nestled in both hands.

"Drop it, Rose!" the Batman shouted. "It's all over now."

"You got *that* right!" the woman shouted back, suddenly shifting her hips and firing a burst at one of the bullies who was cringing against the window of the bar. The bully went down, a dark circle blossoming on his forehead. The Batarang sliced through the night air, wrapping its capture-cord around the woman's ankles and bringing her down. The Batman followed right behind, grabbing the submachine gun out of the redhead's hands before she could fire again.

He quickly secured the woman's hands and feet with restraints. Sirens split the night air—an SQ3 command automatically transmitted the location of wherever the Batmobile was docked to Gotham PD. The Batman got to his feet just as the boom of twin shotgun blasts assaulted his ears. Another of the bullies was down, his chest torn away from the impact. A quick glance told the story—the man Batman thought he had disarmed had tipped over his own wheelchair and then used his massive upper body strength to pull himself over to the shotgun. And he *kept* crawling until he was in position for the kill.

The Batman walked slowly over to where the man with the shotgun lay on the ground. "Gary," the crime fighter said quietly, "it's done now. I know you've got another gun hidden somewhere. Give it up—you'll be no good to Rosie dead."

The man on the ground reached toward his belt, then stopped as four squad cars turned into the street, blocking it at both ends. He nodded his head slowly, as if to acknowledge words of wisdom.

The Batman bent down and reached out one hand. The man he had called Gary grasped the gloved hand. The Batman picked him up with one hand, carried him over to the upended wheelchair, straightened the wheelchair, and gently deposited the man into it. The man looked up at the Batman, then handed over a gleaming chrome .357 Magnum revolver.

Leaving the man in the wheelchair, the Batman walked over to where the police had gathered. He pulled aside a portly man with sergeant's stripes on his uniform and spent a couple of minutes explaining what had occurred. Then, without another word, he touched his utility belt, and the canopy to the Batmobile slid back.

In less than half a minute, the Batman reentered, closed the canopy, and left the scene.

"What in the world was *that* all about?" Debra Kane demanded, leaning forward in her seat.

"What did *you* see?" the crime fighter asked in return.

"I saw a crowd of creeps, hanging out, waiting for someone to push around."

"What else?"

"I saw a woman dressed like some movie version of a prostitute. And a man in a wheelchair. Then it all went crazy. How did you—?"

"I had one major advantage over you," the Batman said. "I've known them for a long time."

"Those creeps hanging around the—?"

"No. Rosie the Riveter and One-Punch Gary. They're partners."

"Partners in what?"

"Murder," the Batman said. "They're professional killers, both of them."

"Then what was—?"

"I don't know yet," the crime fighter replied. "I can tell you this much for sure. At least two of the men in that crew had done something to someone. Something bad. My best guess is rape. And somebody—the victim, her family, friends—hired Rosie and Gary to get revenge. They've worked this bit before. Everybody's eyes are on Rosie so they never see Gary coming."

"I can see why they call her Rosie the Riveter—every

man's eyes were *glued* to her. But the other one, how come—?''

"They don't call her the Riveter because of the way she looks," the Batman said. "It's because of the way she shoots—as neat and precise as a row of rivets. Her reputation is that she never misses. And they call Gary One-Punch because his upper body is incredibly strong. He can immobilize a man with a single blow. And I guarantee that when they get to court, he'll try and take all the weight off Rosie and put it on himself. He may be in a wheelchair, but you can always count on him to stand up."

The Batmobile was back in the shadows of the city, running under the abandoned Gotham Viaduct with its lights off, using the infrared sensors to warn of danger. "I've never been down here after dark before," Debra said.

"Smart move," the Batman replied. "In this part of town, things *are* as bad as they seem."

Both were silent for a few minutes, watching the dots of light where members of the homeless army had built small fires to ward off the evil spirits they were busy ingesting. Occasionally, a hungry dog would flit past in their vision, hunting hungrier rats.

Then Debra Kane leaned forward again. "Can I ask you something else?"

"Yes."

"They . . . knew they were going to be caught, didn't they? I mean, not at first, but when . . . *you* showed up. They couldn't get away then, right?"

"Right."

"So why did they keep on? If they had just stopped, they would still have been arrested, but it wouldn't be for *murder*. And with so many witnesses . . ."

"They're professionals," the Batman said, a grudging but ascertainable note of respect in his voice. "True professionals."

The Batmobile eased to a stop right in front of Debra Kane's apartment building. The canopy slid back as the Batman effortlessly vaulted out of his seat to the ground. He again extended a hand to Debra and gently lifted her out of the vehicle.

She stood on the sidewalk facing the masked man, a torrential stream of conflicting emotions raging through her. "Did you . . . just happen to be there tonight? When that man tried to . . . ?"

"No," the Batman answered. "I wanted to talk to you. About the work you do. About some work I need to do."

"Why . . . me?"

"I know you are a person of deep conviction and sincerity when it comes to your work," the crime fighter replied. "My sources are not important—I know them to be as impeccable as if I had made the observations with my own eyes."

"Would you . . . like to come up?" Debra asked, thinking how thunderstruck her neighbors would be to see the legendary Batman stalking their halls. And thinking about the man under the mask, too. "I could—"

"Yes," the Batman replied, cutting her off. "I would like to come up. There's just one small thing that would make it a bit easier."

"And what's that?" Debra Kane asked.

"Leave a window open," the Batman replied, leaping

back into the Batmobile and pulling away with the canopy still in the open position.

Debra walked up the eight flights to her studio apartment, bypassing the cantankerous old elevator that seemed to delight in trapping unwary tenants between floors. Besides, she told herself ruefully, until she finally managed to put some money together, this was as close to a Stair-Master as she was going to get.

Inside, she carefully latched the door behind her before opening the single back window. She glanced outside at the night, seeing the familiar fire escapes lined with flowerpots the residents used to beautify their surroundings. Occasionally, they also used them to convey their displeasure at noisy activity in the alley below. So many pots had been launched in that fashion over the years that the alley itself was covered with a motley assortment of flowers and vines.

"Should I change my clothes?" Debra wondered to herself. "Do I have time for a shower?" She paced impatiently around the small apartment, trying to decide until the issue was settled by a black shape flowing through her back window.

"I hope my . . . entrance didn't disturb you," the masked man said politely. The dividing line between his dark presence and the room's dim light was impossible to determine.

"Not at all," she replied, as though addressing someone who had unexpectedly telephoned. "Can I get you something?"

"I would appreciate a glass of water," the Batman answered.

Debra Kane opened the refrigerator and twisted the spigot on a plastic bottle of spring water, filling a blue glass nearly to the brim. She brought the glass over to the dark figure still standing in front of her back window.

"Thank you," he said, taking the glass from her hand. As their fingers touched, Debra felt a crackle-joint of electricity shoot up her arm. She quickly glanced up into the opaque masked eyes looking for . . . she didn't know what.

The Batman's body seemed to shift with the fluidity of an ink blot, rearranging itself somewhere behind Debra's sofa. Was that just the hint of a smile that flashed across his lips for a second?

"You said you wanted to . . . talk to me about something?" Debra asked.

"Is it true that there is no biogenetic code for criminality?" he asked without further preliminaries, the need to understand the depth of his mother's contributions paramount in his mind.

"That is *absolutely* true," Debra answered. "The idea of the 'born criminal' or the 'bad seed' has been scientifically disproven for decades. That kind of nonsense is still spouted by people who are opposed to social programs, but—"

"Why?" the Batman interrupted.

"Why? Because if children can be 'born bad,' why spend money on education, or health care, or public housing, or—"

"Child Protective Services?"

"That's *right!*" Debra Kane responded, an undercurrent of anger in her clear professorial voice.

"If criminals are made, not born . . . isn't it true that abused children grow up to be criminals?"

"That's *not* true," Debra snapped, her academic tone vanishing as she responded to the challenge. "Certainly, child abuse contributes to adult criminality, but it's not that simple. There are many other outcomes as well: from eating disorders to drug abuse to suicide."

"But—"

"Let me finish," she interrupted firmly. "There are so many adult negatives associated with child abuse that it would take a textbook to list them all. Child abuse can push two similarly maltreated children in entirely opposite directions. One incest victim becomes promiscuous in adulthood, another never engages in sex again. But most victims don't become criminals."

"But if the abuse was . . . serious enough, couldn't—?"

"What is 'serious' to one person isn't necessarily so to another. You never hear anything about emotional abuse, but in some ways, it is the most damaging of all. The only valid generalization about child abuse is that no generalization is valid."

"I understand," the Batman responded soberly. "What confuses me is this: every time I have questioned a serial killer, child abuse was in his background. So doesn't that mean—?"

"No!" exclaimed Debra, jumping to her feet. "There is *always* a choice. If you excuse a serial killer because he was tortured as a child, you disrespect the thousands and thousands of other children who were treated even worse and yet never, *never* imitated their oppressor. Don't you *dare* do that in my house!"

"I apologize," the masked man said quietly. "I wasn't drawing conclusions, just asking for answers. I'm sorry if

I gave you the wrong impression. I fight crime—that's what I do. At least, that's what I *thought* I was doing. Now I think what I'm doing is fighting *criminals*. And I think you . . . and people like you . . . are fighting crime."

"We are," Debra Kane said. "It's true. We're on the front lines. We see the monsters way before you do. And as best we can, we try to intervene before it's too late."

"I know how truly important your work is," the masked man said, flowing to his feet and extending one gloved hand.

"Thank you," Debra replied.

"Many abused children refuse to imitate the oppressor when they become adults," the Batman said, still holding her hand, bowing his head to whisper. "And some go even further, don't they?"

Debra nodded, not able to speak.

"You have my deepest respect," the Batman whispered. "One warrior's respect for another."

Debra Kane closed her eyes. When she opened them, the Batman was gone.

The Batmobile slowly snaked through Crime Alley, a hunting hawk to the underworld's mice. Word of Batman's latest appearance had already made its way down the whisper-stream—when the Batmobile was loose, the stalkers shivered and the prowlers prayed. Even the more benign street players shuddered involuntarily; the penny-ante pickpockets and popcorn pimps cowered at the bad omen. Once the shadow-camouflaged machine left Crime Alley, its speed increased. On the expressway, the Batmobile slipped through high-speed traffic like a fleeting memory, heading for Cambridge Mews, an exclusive suburb ten miles from the city.

The crime fighter glanced at the video screen. The readout said:

Alexander Horton, 7 Plebiscite Lane

He tapped a single key, and the screen changed to a street map. The target address was marked with a blinking red arrow. Batman nodded grimly, then tapped the same key again. The pixels on the video screen broke and reassembled, finally showing a photographic image of the house, a substantial home in the Mediterranean style. Architecturally undistinguished, the house, like many of its neighbors, was completely surrounded by a wrought iron fence. The fence around the target house was different, however. Unlike the decorative style favored by others, this fence was all business. And, the Batman noted, approximately three times the height of typical fences, about fifteen feet. As the video image expanded, he could make out a thin coil of yellow and black wire entwined around the top of the fence—even if a burglar were tempted to scale such a height, one touch anywhere around the top would cause immediate death by electrocution.

As the Batmobile neared its target, the masked man tripped a toggle switch marked E2. Instantly the huge machine switched from turbine to electric power. Originally designed as an emergency backup in case of turbine failure, a set of special storage batteries held a charge sufficient to power the Batmobile for about forty-five minutes at speeds up to fifty miles per hour.

Still another use was the ability to move in absolute silence.

Continuing to reference the video screen while piloting the Batmobile, the masked man did one full circuit of the area, noting a steep drop-off behind the target house. He also marked the presence of a bulky man standing just inside the front gate—the only opening to the grounds.

One more circuit completed the reconnaissance. He docked the Batmobile in a thicket of woods that ran behind the row of houses, using the machine's full-time all-wheel drive and special-compound tires to negotiate the broken terrain with ease. Exiting the Batmobile, the masked man found himself looking up at the fence that ran behind the back of the target house. He stood as still as the surrounding trees, feeling the atmosphere with his senses as a blind man reads Braille. After a full five minutes, he took a large, flat, circular object about the diameter of a tire from the Batmobile's storage bin and held it in two hands against his chest. The masked man snapped both wrists out sharply—four black aluminum legs popped out. The Batman anchored the legs in the soft ground—they were of two different lengths, so the flat circular top was now at an angle. The masked man knelt, carefully adjusting the disc. Finally he nodded, as if in agreement with an indisputable truth.

The Batman turned and started up the steep slope. When he reached the fence, he turned, facing back toward the woods. He took a deep, cleansing breath through his nose and leaped into space. The natural elevation propelled him in a long arc, precisely at the center of the waiting disc. He landed with both feet and was immediately launched back in the direction from which he came— the black circular object was a mini-trampoline. The dark figure passed over the fence as undetectably as the night itself. A midair flip landed the Batman on all fours—he was inside the compound.

Thanks to decades of training, the night-rider's eyes adjusted as instantly as a cat's. With the sole exception of a soft, rosy glow from a corner room on the third story, the house was as dark as the outside grounds.

But after a quick glance, the Batman moved away from the glow, heading for the front of the house.

The gate guard was monstrous—a man of sumo wrestler proportions, with no discernible neck. Disabling a man of that size without killing him would require surgical precision . . . and a good deal of luck. The Batman mentally sorted through his options. Then a gloved hand flashed to his utility belt, emerging with three identical clear glass balls. The Batman shifted the three balls between his fingers, seeking that perfect symmetry that would put him in harmony with the objects. He looked down from his perch above the sumo guard and flung his hand forward, sailing all three balls in a perfect triangle. The leading ball struck the sumo on top of his head. The other two hit the ground, one on each side of the huge man. The sumo swooned. Then he fell to the ground with a noise like a safe hitting a putting green.

The Batman moved in, checking for vital signs with a thumb against the carotid artery. The sumo wore a red knit shirt with the name "Leo" sewn in neat script over the heart. He would be out for at least an hour. When he woke up, he would be nursing a spinal-tap headache for a couple of days. After that, he'd be as bad as new.

The Batman turned and headed for the house, a shadow among shadows.

Even seated, one could see that the tall man still had the remnants of a physique which once intimidated street criminals by its mere presence. The man stood almost six and a half feet, weighing nearly three hundred pounds, and his tiny head exaggerated his body to almost comic-book proportions. His small, close-set eyes were as flat and depthless as a lizard's, but his hands were busy. A busty blonde stood before him, dressed only in a bright red silk kimono. The man had one end of the kimono's belt in a huge hand—he was pulling on it with the gleeful expression of a child unwrapping a Christmas gift.

"You like your present?" he asked the blonde.

"Oh, you *know* I do, Alex," she squealed. "It's beautiful," she said, her lacquered nails toying with the diamond choker around her slender neck.

"Well how about letting me *see* it then?" he mock-snarled, still pulling at the kimono belt.

"Just give me a minute, I'll . . ."

The blonde's voice died in her throat as a pool of shadow in one corner of the living room materialized into the shape of a giant bat. The huge man came to his feet with a speed that belied his size. "What the hell happened to—?"

"Leo?" the Batman replied. "You don't have to worry about him—he's gone to sleep on the job."

"Yeah? Well, let's see if you—" The big man drew a pistol from his kidney holster but dropped it unfired as the Batman stabbed a two-finger nerve block to the inside of his elbow. Unarmed but still dangerous, the big man launched his trademark left hook—the punch that had immobilized a whole generation of thugs—but the Batman slipped inside the punch and drove his gloved fist to the big man's heart, followed by a quick series of three-finger kites that climbed from the waist to the throat. The big man staggered back, desperately searching for a weapon, but the Batman's paralyzing heel strike to the sternum ended the unequal contest.

The blonde's mouth was agape, but no sound came out. Her red kimono popped open, but she didn't notice, watching entranced as the Batman looped the flexible restraints around the big man's wrists and ankles. The blonde gasped as the masked man picked up his huge adversary in two hands and dumped him unceremoniously into the armchair he had so pleasurably occupied only minutes before.

"Please sit down," the Batman told her, one gloved finger pointing to a chrome barstool with a padded red seat. The stool was behind the restrained man in the easy chair. His words were polite, but clearly offered no alternative.

The blonde sat stiffly on the stool, hastily pulling her kimono closed. "What did you do to—?"

"Nothing of consequence," the Batman assured her. "He'll be conscious in another minute or two." The opaque discs covering his eyes seemed to glow as he regarded the woman's face. "I am going to talk to this . . . man," the Batman said. "He is going to answer my questions. Then I am going to leave. I'm sorry about this, but you . . . must remain where you are until I'm finished. I give you my word that you will not be injured. Do you understand?"

"Yes," the blonde said quietly. "Look, you're not going to . . . *torture* him or anything, are you?"

"No," the Batman replied, popping open a pouch in his utility kit and quickly assembling some small items on a coffee table near the armchair. Approaching the seated man, the Batman touched a nerve cluster at the junction between the man's jaw and neck. Instantly the tiny eyes popped open, and the big man surged in vain against the restraints.

"What do you want?" he snarled.

"I want some answers," the Batman replied. "And I want them tonight."

"What if I—?"

"I'm not here to bargain," the masked man said. "I am going to ask you some questions. You are going to answer those questions."

"And then you're out of here?" the big man asked.

"Yes."

"Ask away, pal," the big man said, a ghastly smile slashing across his porcine face.

"Joe Chill," the Batman said quietly. "Who paid you to kill him?"

"*Kill* him? What the hell are you talking about?" the big man demanded. "He was a wanted man. A murderer, for god's sake. I was trying to arrest him. He went for his gun. I didn't have a choice."

"He was hit with seven rounds from a nine-millimeter pistol," the Batman said.

"Yeah, that's right. Regulation all the way."

"No, it wasn't. The caliber was regulation, not the bullets. You used hollow-points. With mercury tips."

"Hey, a lot of cops use hot loads, pal. It's a war out there."

"I won't ask you again," the masked man said. "I know about Barbara Jane Slocum. I know about you. If you don't tell me voluntarily, I have other . . . things I could use."

"Truth serum? Don't waste your time, pal. My mind is too strong. I could lie to a polygraph and never bounce the needles. Believe me, I know."

"You *are* going to tell me," the Batman said. "That's a promise. Now if you—"

"Wait!" the big man said, his brain racing, his survival instincts on full boil. "All you want is the information?"

"Yes," the Batman replied.

"And if I talk, it's off the record? You swear?"

"You have my word of honor."

"And if I was to . . . implicate myself somehow, it wouldn't go anywhere."

"It won't leave this room," the Batman said. "I'll give you five minutes, no more. Then you can start talking or we can see if your mind is as strong as you claim."

"I don't *need* no five minutes," the big man said, chuckling inwardly. "I know your word is good. Hell, everyone knows that. Go ahead, ask me your questions."

"Why did you murder Joe Chill?"

"It was a job, pal—a job I got paid to do, that's all."

"Who paid you?"

"The Slocum bitch, just like you figured."

"Why?"

"Why *what*?"

"Why did Slocum want Chill murdered?"

"He did a job for . . . them. And the cops were closing in. They was afraid he'd turn yellow and give them up."

"Slowly now," the Batman said, his voice dropping a half octave. "What was the job Chill did?"

"It was a hit," the big man said. "Went smooth as silk, too—all the cops thought it was a street mugging gone wrong, just like it was planned."

"Who was the target?" the masked man said, leaning forward, his voice slightly fluttery around the edges.

"Some nosy society bitch. Martha Wayne, I think her name was. She was getting in the way."

"The way of what?" the Batman asked, outwardly winning the war for self-control that raged within him.

"Look, pal, you got any *idea* how much money there is in kiddie porn? Well, let me tell you, neither did I. There was a real sweet organization set up. It was so easy. I mean, look at the product. It's not like drugs—the more you step on cocaine, the weaker and weaker it gets, right? Well, with this kiddie porn stuff, you can make copies *endlessly,* understand? It was worth a fortune. And the beauty part is nobody knew about it, see? I mean, I was a *cop*, right? And *I* never heard of it. I mean . . . I *heard* of it, but just . . . rumors, like. Nothing big-time."

"Go on," the Batman said quietly.

"At first, all they wanted was some tips. This Martha Wayne, she was feeding information direct to Headquarters. Where she got it, I don't know—that dame had some *good* sources, that was for sure. Anyway, all I had to do was let Barbara Jane know when a raid was coming down. That worked good for a while, but finally they said this Wayne broad was going to be a problem *forever*, you understand what I mean?"

"Oh yes," the Batman replied.

"So the word went out. To hit her, I mean. This Joe Chill, he was supposed to be a real pro. And he pulled it off, I give him that. But after a while, he got scared. I don't know of what . . . he never said. He was . . . spooking at shadows, like—talking about ghosts and stuff like that. So I . . . did him. He didn't suspect a thing."

"You killed Slocum too?"

"Yeah. Had to do it. The top guy, the one who was calling all the shots, he said it was her or me."

"The top guy?"

"Her uncle. Or anyway, that's what she called him. Malady, his name is. But he split a long time ago. I heard he went to Europe or something."

"You knew what you were doing?"

"Yeah. Well . . . what do you mean?"

"You knew these . . . people were raping children? And taking pictures of it to sell?"

"Well . . . yeah. I mean, I wouldn't do anything like that *myself*. I mean, I'm not into kids or anything. Far as I'm concerned, they're a bunch of perverts."

"Lieutenant Alexander Horton," the Batman said softly. "Didn't that job, that rank . . . mean anything to you?"

"Don't go all gooey on me," the big man sneered. "I was for sale. So, big deal. Hell, *lots* of people are for sale. Just like her . . ." he said, tilting his head backward to indicate the blonde. "You trying to say I'm the only bent cop you ever heard of?"

"No. But you're the first that would help people rape children."

"You want anything else?"

"No," the Batman said. "I have enough."

"You promised . . ."

The Batman walked past the restrained man as if he were a piece of furniture, addressing himself to the blonde. "Here is the key for the restraints," he said. "You can unlock them anytime after I leave."

The blonde sat rock-still in the chair, not moving.

"Do you understand?" the Batman asked.

The blonde didn't move.

"Hey, you stupid bitch, pay attention!" Horton snapped. "You forget you're a whore or something? Get off your fat butt and let me out of these things."

The blonde's eyes came into focus. She looked into the Batman's masked face and nodded.

The Batman vanished as suddenly as he had appeared.

"What a chump!" the big man laughed. "Best deal I ever made. When the Batman says something is off the record, he *can't* go to the law with it—everybody on the street knows his word is good as gold. All I need is a little time. Before he even *starts* tracking down all that stuff I told him, I'll be on the beach in Rio. Hey, Ronda, what are you doing? I told you to get over here and cut me loose."

The big man's head twisted on his thick neck, but he couldn't catch a glimpse of the blonde. "Where the hell did you go?" he snapped angrily.

"Me, I'm right here," the blonde said quietly, stepping into view, holding the pistol she had recovered from the floor in one hand. "*You're* the one who's going."

"Focus!" the Batman commanded, stalking the floor of his cave. "In combat, anger is the enemy," he chanted to himself, the words of his first *sensei,* internalized when Bruce Wayne was still a child.

A child without a childhood.

A boy who would become more than a man—and, as if in payment, also become less.

Suddenly the Batman whirled, his cape flowing behind him as smoothly as an afterimage. Snatching a telephone, he punched a single button and waited for the response, his uncowled face as expressionless as any mask could be.

"Yes?" came a voice through the receiver. There was no need for a greeting on either end of the dedicated line. Only one person would ever call—only one person would ever answer.

"Do you have anyone who has experience with pedophiles?" the Batman asked.

"I have quite a few . . . unfortunately," Commissioner Gordon added. "Specifically, what do you need?"

"Someone who tracks them as they track children. Someone with experience in counterterrorism."

"I know just the man," the commissioner responded. "He's a bit . . . unconventional, but there's nobody better."

"Name?"

"Trask. Sherwood Trask. He works both Probation and Parole. Everything from pre-sentence investigations to track-downs. Been doing it for a long time. In fact, he runs some of the training sessions at the academy."

"Would he know anything about Leonard Tuxley?"

"The guy they found in the tunnel at Hellgate? Sure. In fact, I was just going over that file—Trask is your man all right."

"Can you ask him to meet with me?"

"Yes. Give me a callback, say in half an hour?"

"Done," the Batman said, breaking the connection.

The Batmobile entered the highway from its place of concealment, merging with the traffic stream, heading for Gotham. The night-rider drove with shrouded lights, relying on the sonar system and his own ability to pilot the vehicle under minimum-visibility conditions. The video screen scrolled data on the man he was about to meet.

Trask, Sherwood
d.o.b. 8/16/44 (51) 5′4″/156/BRN/BLU
B.A., CJ, GCC, 1966
M.A., CM, GCC, 1988

A college graduate majoring in Criminal Justice at Gotham City. A master's degree in criminology twenty-two years later? The Batman frowned at the disparity between the two dates, but the next scroll answered his unspoken question:

> *U.S. Army. 87th Infantry. Vietnam, 1967–1969. Bronze*
> *Stars (2), Purple Heart (1)*
> *Gotham P.D., 1970–*
> *Current Assignment: Commander, Intensive Supervision*
> *Team*
> *Departmental Commendations: 21*

The Batman opened the file and discovered that Trask had been decorated for everything from heroism under fire to tracking down a serial child molester.

> *Departmental Disciplinary Proceedings: 4*

This file showed four separate civilian complaints, all involving excessive force. Two of the complaints had been referred to a grand jury. Trask had never been indicted, nor had disciplinary action against him ever been sustained.

Docking the Batmobile in its luxurious hiding place, the Batman took to the rooftops, heading for a six-story tenement in the Bowery. As he approached, he could see a flash of white against the dark roof. "As agreed," he thought to himself, sweeping down to land.

As the Batman touched down, he saw the figure of a man slouched against a shack on the roof. The flash of white was a T-shirt, worn under an old army jacket. The slouching man's arms were folded over a deep, wide chest. As the Batman approached, the arms unfolded, revealing a pistol in each hand. The man was no longer slouching— and the pistols looked at home in his hands.

The Batman bowed slightly. "Sherwood Trask?" he asked.

The man he was facing returned the bow. As he did, it became apparent his entire head was shaved—his skull gleamed in the night. "Say a number," the muscular man demanded.

"Twenty-nine," the Batman replied, repeating the signal the commissioner had given Trask.

"Okay." Trask nodded. The pistols vanished as quickly as they had appeared. Trask stuck out his right hand. The Batman shook it. "What do you want to know?" Trask asked.

The Batman moved closer, dropping his voice almost below audibility. "What can you tell me about Leonard Tuxley?"

"He's a chronic child molester—"

"A pedophile?"

"No," the investigator replied, "not a 'pedophile.' That's *their* word, not ours."

"I don't understand," the Batman said.

"Their whole game is about euphemisms," Trask answered, his voice as level as if he were reading a road map. "They don't call what they do child molestation, they call it 'intergenerational love.' The definition of 'pedophile' is 'lover of children,' understand?"

The Batman nodded, remembering his conversation with Debra Kane. "I didn't mean to interrupt," he said. "Please go on."

"Here's the real deal," the investigator said, his pale blue eyes locked onto the opaque discs in the Batman's cowl. "Tuxley was busted for molesting at least half a dozen little boys. He's a computer expert. That's how he got access to the kids—he was a private tutor. I say at least half a dozen because that's how many eventually came forward—we expect there were more. A lot more. Anyway, Tuxley pleaded guilty. His lawyer said it was to spare the kids the trauma of testifying—what he wanted was to spare Tuxley the trauma of prison. The judge said Tuxley was a sick man—he was wrong on both counts. But that didn't matter. The judge decided Tuxley needed treatment, not prison. And there was this program that said it could work wonders with guys like Tuxley. Bottom line? He got psychiatric probation."

"But he was in prison when—"

"Yeah, he was. Finally. But he didn't go right to the joint. What happened was we violated him."

"Violated?"

"Yeah. He violated the terms and conditions of his probation. That's about the only hold we have on those guys. We can't make the courts send them to prison, but we sure as hell can make them walk a straight line when they're under our supervision."

"He molested another child?"

"No—at least not so far as we know. But there's always conditions of probation that degenerates can't handle. Like, for incest offenders, one of the conditions is that there has to be a lock on the bathroom door."

"Why would that—?"

"Incest is all about *power*," Trask said. "It's all about *control*, see? One of the ways they establish their dominance is to tell the child . . . *their* child . . . that there's no privacy. No privacy means no safety."

"What was Tuxley's condition?"

"No videotaping children. That was his 'hobby.' He'd go to Little League games or a kids' ice-skating contest. The activity didn't matter—he wanted video footage of kids."

"Why?"

"I told you—he's a computer expert. What he'd do was to digitalize the tape, break it down into tiny units. Then he could electronically rearrange the units, depending on what computer keys you would touch."

"I still don't see why—"

"It's the latest thing," the cop told the Batman. "Interactive kiddie porn. Pictures of the kid come up on your video monitor. You tap the right keys, the kid does whatever you want. Or you can put yourself in the picture too."

The night-rider took a deep breath through his nose, trying to clear his head. "Officer Trask, if you—"

"Woody," the muscular cop said. "That's what they call me."

"Woody, then," the Batman said. "So Tuxley was in Hellgate because he violated his probation?"

"Not exactly," the cop replied. "When we violated him, he was videotaping a gymnastic meet for kids ten and under. And they *did* put him away, but not at Hellgate. They sent him to a minimum-security joint. That's where he supposedly got 'rehabilitated.' He only did about a third of his sentence, then he was paroled."

"And then?"

"And then the Intensive Supervision Team went back into action. We work both ends: probation if they avoid a prison sentence, parole if they don't. We're always around. When we hit Tuxley's house we hit the jackpot—he had boxes of kiddie porn in the basement. He even had a computerized list of every photograph. The miserable maggot had his computer crash-coded, but we managed to find our way in without nuking the data."

"Did he . . . take the photos himself?"

"We don't know yet. We locked him up on a PV— parole violation—so he had to go back and serve the rest of his sentence. We were still going through his stash when we got word that he'd been shanked. It'll take months to sort through it all.''

"Investigations, arrests,'' the Batman mused out loud. ''I thought probation officers ... parole officers ... I thought what you did was a form of social work.''

''For some, it is,'' the cop replied. ''Especially with juveniles. And for a lot of our clients, we can do some real good. Sometimes all a guy needs is a job. Or to stop drinking. Or a high school education. They want help, we can usually give it to them. But the IST isn't about rehabilitation, it's about protection of society. We work with the stone recidivists. We *expect* problems. And we're ready to deal with them when they surface.''

''I was told that Tuxley would have known something about kiddie sex tours. Did he—?''

''You mean the deal with Udon Khai?'' the cop responded. ''No question about it. Tuxley did go on one of the tours. We overheard him talking to one of his freak friends, bragging about how great it was over there.''

''I'm surprised he would be that indiscreet.''

''Well, he was talking on his home phone,'' the cop smiled. ''I guess he had some expectation of privacy.''

''You mean you ... ?''

''Sure.''

''But you're a police officer. How could you—?''

''Hey, pal.'' The cop laughed. ''Let me get this straight: you're calling *me* a vigilante?''

The Batman took one step back, then bowed slightly, as though acknowledging a great truth. Then he went back into the night.

Three days later, a jumbo jet lifted off from Gotham International Airport. Flight 67 to San Francisco was right on time. Bruce Wayne had been one of the last to board, sliding into seat 2-G undisturbed. He always took a window seat in first class—it minimized the prospect of interaction with other passengers, especially on long flights.

The little brunette stewardess was used to passengers whose idea of "flirting" was to stare at her legs or make crudely suggestive remarks. She never let it bother her— "Just part of the job," she thought to herself. The blandly handsome man in 2-G was a surprise. "Not that he actually *ignored* me," she said to her roommate that evening, "it was more like I wasn't there at all."

"Maybe he was just preoccupied," the roommate said. "You know, big businessman and all."

"Maybe so," the stewardess said, unconvinced.

Bruce Wayne caught a cab at the airport. The cab took him to the Cheshire Hotel. He waited patiently at the reception desk until a clerk detached himself from an animated conversation with a young woman in a waitress outfit and strolled over. "Can I help you?" he asked.

"I have a reservation," Bruce Wayne began when he was interrupted by the clerk slapping a bell on the countertop and shouting "Front!" at the same time.

"That won't be necessary—" Bruce Wayne started to say, but it was too late—a husky bellman was already at his side, bending forward to wrap his hand around the handle to Bruce Wayne's large alligator suitcase. The bellman straightened up. A jolt of pain shot across his face. "What the hell is in—?"

"A set of weights," Bruce Wayne said casually. "For working out. I always carry them on the road with me."

"Wow!" the bellman said, impressed despite himself. "I mean, the guy was big all right, but not *that* big," he told a couple of other bellmen when they were all on their break. "Fact is, he looked kind of . . . I don't know . . . *soft* maybe. But he picked that suitcase up like it was nothing."

Inside his suite, Bruce Wayne unpacked with great care, assembling various items on a long tray of white ceramic. He used a hand-held scanner to sweep the interior for eavesdropping devices, then checked the windows for potential access from outside. It was forty minutes before he picked up the tray and walked into the bathroom. In another forty minutes, another man walked out.

The other man was older than Bruce Wayne. Heavier too. His hair was slicked back from his forehead, revealing a jagged scar on his right temple. His brown eyes were set in a round, almost Oriental face.

The man replaced the tray inside the alligator suitcase and twirled the combination lock tumblers after he snapped it shut. Then he picked up the receiver and punched a number into the keypad.

"Safe House," a voice answered.

"Could I speak to Deadly Dave?" the man asked.

"Who should I say is calling?" the voice responded.

"Big Jack Hollister," the man in the hotel said.

In less than a minute, a man's voice came on the line. "This is Dave," he said.

"Big Jack Hollister. I understand you're expecting my call?"

"I might be . . . who *gave* you that understanding?"

"Victor C."

"Good enough. What can I do for you?"

"I need some of your time, that's all."

"Do you know the Lavender Dragon?"

"I can find it."

"Anytime after ten tonight. Just ask for me at the bar."

The man who called himself Big Jack Hollister flagged down a cab. When it pulled to the curb, he climbed into the backseat. "Do you know where the Lavender Dragon is?" he asked the driver.

"Yeah, sure. But look . . . I mean, it ain't none of my business, but that joint is only for—"

"You're right," Big Jack said in a flinty voice. "It ain't none of your business."

The rest of the trip was blissfully quiet as the cabbie sulked in silence. His sulking changed to anger when the passenger handed him exact change. "What's the matter, pal," he sneered. "A little tip's gonna break you?"

"You got a problem?" Big Jack said quietly, leaning back inside the cab. "You wanna come out here and discuss it?"

The cab took off, tires squealing.

The man who called himself Big Jack entered the club. He carefully worked his way through a maze of mostly male bodies, not responding to offers to buy him a drink. When he reached his destination, he waited calmly until a man wearing a bright yellow T-shirt and a leather apron leaned on the bar and asked, "What'll it be?"

"Deadly Dave. He's expecting me. Name's Big Jack."

"Well, I can see *that*," the bartender said. He winked at Big Jack and moved off. He was back in a minute. Again he leaned over the bar. "Last booth on the right," he said, pointing toward the back of the bar.

Big Jack walked over to the booth. It was occupied by one man—a man with delicate features and hard eyes. He stood as Big Jack approached. The two men shook hands wordlessly. In response to a wave of Dave's hand, the other man sat down.

"Tell me what you need," Dave said.

Matching the other man's let's-get-down-to-it tone, Big Jack asked, "You know about a man named Drako? He lives on a yacht in the Dragonfire Marina over on—"

"Yeah. I know him," Dave replied, his voice thick with contempt. "I know his name, and I know his game."

"Is it true he sets up kiddie sex tours? To Udon Khai?"

"Sure it's true. Why do you think he named his yacht the *Lollypop*? He's not only sleaze, he's proud of it."

"Do you know a man named William X. Malady?"

"Never heard of him."

"You know anybody who has actually gone on one of those sex tours?"

"I know *of* such people."

"Meaning?"

Dave leaned forward. "Meaning that people who have sex with children are degenerate scum, okay? Meaning that there's nothing *homosexual* about men having sex with boys. Meaning that those filthy pedophiles are always trying to throw in with us . . . always trying to make it an issue of sexual liberation instead of what it really is."

"Which is?"

"A crime," Dave said flatly. "A despicable crime. If you know Victor C., you know how we feel about it."

"I need to go over there," the man who called himself Big Jack said quietly. "What can you tell me about the operation?"

"They screen real carefully," Dave replied. "If you get past that, whatever you can pay for, you get."

"How much?"

"Depends on what you want. Cheapest is just for passage into the country. See, Udon Khai has a tight visa policy—normally the wait is about six months for clearance. But if you go over on one of Drako's little tours, you can get a visa that same day. So if all you want is to buy a ticket to Pedophile Paradise, you can do it for around ten grand, everything included."

"What's 'everything'?"

"Not what you think," Dave answered. "It just means a round-trip ticket and four nights at a hotel. Anything extra, you have to find for yourself."

"Or—?"

"Or you can have it all brought to you. That's twenty-five and up, depending on what you want to do."

"With a child?"

"Yes, with a child. What do you think we're talking about here, Club Med?"

"Sorry. I didn't mean to offend. It just seems so . . . impossible to me."

"That's their camouflage," Dave replied. "And it works pretty good."

"So all it takes is money—"

"—and connections."

"And connections, right. Then I *could* go on one of those tours?"

"I don't think so," Dave said quietly. "They have one final requirement—the Acid Test, they call it."

"What's that?"

"You don't want to know."

"You mean—?"

"Yeah. You have to . . . have sex with a child. They supply the child. And they videotape it. That way, they know you're the real thing. And that you won't talk if anything goes wrong."

The man who called himself Big Jack closed his eyes, as though to banish the hideous images. A waiter came over to the booth. Catching Big Jack's eye, Dave ordered for the two of them. "Two tuna on pita."

"Anything from the bar?" the waiter asked.

"Water," Dave said. "Tap water. No ice."

Neither man said anything until the waiter came back with their order.

"Thank you," Big Jack said.

"Don't thank me, thank Victor C.," Dave said. "He's my brother."

"You mean your—?"

"No. Not my bio-brother. A brother I chose. Do you understand?"

"Yes," said Big Jack. Thinking of the children his mother would never have. Of the brothers and sisters he would never have. And of how much the ever-faithful Alfred had given up as well.

Dave took a deep drink from his glass of water. "Anything else I can tell you?"

"Why do they call you Deadly Dave?"

"I used to box when I was a kid. Strictly amateur, but I was pretty good at it."

"Why did you stop?"

"The real fights aren't in some prize ring," Dave said. "And the real fighters aren't there either."

At 1:13 A.M., a phone number was punched into the keypad of the phone in Bruce Wayne's San Francisco hotel room. But it wasn't Bruce Wayne making the call. It wasn't Big Jack Hollister either.

"The plans are changed," the Batman spoke into the receiver. "The tour route is off—I have to go in alone. Would you pull Udon Khai up on the mainframe so that I can get some questions answered?"

"Certainly, sir," Alfred answered, as alert after midnight as he was at the break of day. After a seven-second wait, Alfred spoke. "I have the information on the screen. Awaiting questions."

"Do you have a step-reference map available?" the Batman asked.

"Searching . . . yes!"

"Can you beam it over on frequency four?"

"Are you set up to receive?" Alfred asked.

"Yes," the Batman replied, his eyes going to the open suitcase where a cellular phone rested in a cradle between a tiny liquid crystal screen and a three-inch-wide plain-paper laser printer.

"Stand by," Alfred said.

The Batman eyed the data-port, watching as the diagrammatic representation scrolled past, too fast to read. The plain-paper laser printer was spooling as well. When it finally stopped, the Batman quickly pulled the paper strips, tore them where indicated, and fastened them to the corkboard that backed the inside of the suitcase. He studied the maps for a long minute, sipping from a glass of water as he did so.

The map showed a triangular-shaped area at the intersection of Myanmar, Laos, and Thailand. Its topography was generally mountainous, with a number of plateaus. The Mekong River flowed through the small country, with numerous tributaries clearly shown on the map. The Batman referenced the scale at the bottom of the map, quickly calculating in his head that the country was roughly ten thousand square miles, with the average elevation being six thousand feet above sea level. In tiny print in the lower right corner of the map, the Batman read:

Notes:
(1) Coordinates: 21.54°N   99.00°E
(2) Myanmar formerly called Burma

The crime fighter took a breath. "General data?" he asked.

"The official name of the country is the Kingdom of Udon Khai," Alfred said, "apparently reflecting an older form of government."

"What is the *current* form of government?"

"A military dictatorship," Alfred said dryly. "The third such regime in succession."

"Population?" the Batman queried.

"Very sparse, sir. A total of perhaps four hundred thousand people, four hundred and fifty at the most. This works out to a density of forty-one per square mile. That is an average, of course. It varies from a low of eleven in the highlands to a high of sixty-five hundred in the capital."

"Which is?"

"Mae Ngao. Located within a short drive from the airport. Population is approximately two hundred and fifty thousand."

"What else?"

"Udon Khai has a three-season climate. No winters. It is subject to monsoons, but less so than its neighbors. As you can see from the map, it is landlocked. There are access roads across all three borders, but no information on such roads can be considered secure."

"Because?"

"Guerilla activity," Alfred replied. "The area is almost permanently unstable. The safest entry point is General Pol Xan Rho Airport. This is an ultramodern facility that can accommodate aircraft of any size, up to and including the SST and long-range fighter-bombers."

"How does the country maintain itself?"

"Not very well, sir," Alfred replied. "Per capita income is less than one hundred and fifty dollars per year. They import almost everything: petroleum products, small machinery, motor vehicles, heavy equipment, chemicals, home appliances, medical supplies, assault weapons, military hardware . . . shall I go on?"

"No. Do they export anything at all?"

"Teak is the principal export. And even that valuable resource is being rapidly depleted—they have no conservation or replenishment plan in place."

"What do they grow there?"

"Udon Khai has significant crops of coffee, tobacco, and rice, with lesser amounts of cotton. There are tin deposits, and some jade as well. The teakwood, as I said before. And, of course, poppies."

"For opium?"

"Yes sir. Next to tourism, opium is the country's biggest cash producer. When the 'tourism' file is opened, the computer says—"

"I know what it says about that," the Batman said softly.

"Very well, sir. Will there be anything else?"

"Yes. What can you tell me about the government?"

"In conventional Western terms, there isn't much to speak of," Alfred said. "The current dictator is one General Lin Fa Ngum. There is a large standing army of almost twenty thousand. No navy, of course. Their air force concentrates on short-strike capability—Harrier Jump-Jets and Bell LOH helicopters—all their wars are either internal or near their borders, mostly with drug lords. There had been a tacit agreement between the government and various warlords to share in the opium profits, but once this became commonly known, foreign aid was drastically cut. One of the principal warlords has been targeted for assassination by the military dictatorship—if captured alive, there is no doubt he would implicate the current leadership. Politically, there is complete press censorship. One television channel, one radio transmitter, one newspaper. The rebels occasionally broadcast on an outlaw radio band, but that is sporadic."

"Who are the rebels?"

"The official party line is that there *are* no rebels. All the attacks are attributed to communist forces from one of the surrounding countries. With the breakup of the Soviet Empire, this explanation is not especially plausible. The best information indicates that the rebels are made up of young people who fled the cities for the mountains . . . and even that information cannot be considered reliable."

"Are religious leaders involved in the rebel movement?"

"That is impossible to determine at this time," Alfred said. "The official religion is Theravada Buddhism, but Animism is practiced among some of the mountain tribes."

"Currency?"

"The official unit is the klong. Exchange rate is six hundred and twenty-seven klong per US dollar at close of business yesterday. The currency is highly unstable," Alfred cautioned, "and trafficking in foreign currencies is a crime punishable by death."

"They have the death penalty for currency trading?" the Batman asked, a note of incredulity in his voice.

"They have the death penalty for eighty-seven separate offenses," Alfred said quietly. "It is quite a popular governmental response in Udon Khai."

"What is their language?"

"Udon—the same as the country's name—is the dominant language for diplomatic purposes. French is taught in schools, but only the middle class can afford to send its children. And since English is the common commercial language and almost all members of the middle class are merchants in one form or another, the French isn't used except to impress others. Some of the mountain tribes are alleged to speak in unrecorded dialects, but data is difficult to come by."

"Because . . . ?"

"Because speaking any language other than Udon outside the capital's limits is a crime."

"Punishable by death?"

"Yes sir. Punishable by death. Udon Khai *claims* a literacy rate of twenty-two percent. Unbiased estimates place it much lower. Virtually none of the mountain tribes can read or write."

"Do we own anything nearby?"

"The closest we have is Sydney, Australia, sir. From there, it is a relatively short hop into Udon Khai. I can arrange for use of a private airstrip not far from Mae Ngao."

"Is that where the 'tourists'—?"

"Yes," Alfred said, his voice flat. "Will there be anything else, sir?"

"I need someone who speaks the language," the Batman said. "They must speak fluently enough to do simultaneous translation, and they must be familiar with idiomatic speech."

"Very well, sir. Contact me when you get to Sydney— I should have it all in place by then."

"Thank you, old friend."

"Good hunting, sir," Alfred said, a blood-thickened edge to his usually dry voice.

Bruce Wayne boarded an international flight nonstop to Sydney, his Australian visa in his pocket. In the privacy of his seat, he examined a strip of computer paper Alfred had beamed over to him a few hours before. Captioned "Udon Khai—Dates of Significance," Alfred's research read in chronological order:

1287: Invaded by the Mongols of Kublai Khan.

1654: Portugal establishes Christian mission.

1824: Annexed to British India.

1883: British sell controlling interest to France.

1937: Agreement with France gave some self-rule. Alfred had hand typed "purely illusory" after that entry.

1942: Occupied by Japan.

1949: Became a sovereign nation, democracy established.

1950: Army seized complete control of government.

1973: Popular revolt, democracy reestablished.

1975: Cambodian Communists invade through Laos.

1977: Army, under leadership of General Pol Xan Rho, repels Cambodian forces and again assumes complete control of government.

1988: General Lin Fa Ngum seizes power from General Pol Xan Rho, who hands over the reins in a TV broadcast and is never seen again. The country's airport is renamed in his honor. General Lin Fa Ngum forges closer ties with Western nations, the US and Canada in particular.

1991: The child-sex industry supplants opium as the country's major producer of hard currency.

"Alfred would have made a great journalist," the Batman mused to himself. "He would have made a great *anything* . . . but he gave up his dreams, gave up his whole life to protect me."

Bruce Wayne closed his eyes, but it was the Batman who slept.

And it was the Batman who placed the transpacific call from Bruce Wayne's suite on the top floor of the Barrier Reef Hotel in Sydney.

"Anything new?" he asked.

"Drako's yacht left port thirteen days ago," Alfred said. "According to our sources, he is headed for Udon Khai."

"You have an ETA?"

"Not a precise one, but he should be relatively close even as we speak. You have clearance to land at General Pol Xan Rho Airport tomorrow evening, any time between twenty-one hundred hours and midnight *their* time. Once you are airborne, signal me and I will transmit the landing coordinates—no flight plan need be filed."

"Did you clear the path with the G-Man?" the Batman asked. The G-Man was a Chicago teenager named Gino, also known as the Wizard of Weather. The young man ran a specialized service, furnishing weather predictions for any area of the world in microdetail. Although he used the same satellite data as the commercial weather services, he had devised an interlocking series of complex formulas that squeezed the last drop of accuracy from existing data. The entrepreneurial end of the enterprise was handled by his younger brother Nicholas, known throughout the city's basketball courts as Nick the Quick. Together the two brothers had virtually cornered the narrow-forecast market worldwide.

"Of course I did," Alfred replied, not a trace of asperity in his voice. "I have been assured that the tsunami off the coast of Thailand will, in fact, dissipate itself somewhere in the Indian Ocean. It should be clear and cloudless all the way in."

"Thank you, my friend. Anything else?"

"Yes sir. Your translator is in place. His name is Rhama Bgyn. He will meet your plane and stay with you until your work is completed."

"Will that day ever come?" the crime fighter asked the spirits.

The answer did not comfort him.

Big Jack Hollister piloted the rental car with the ease of a traffic veteran despite the unfamiliarity of right-hand drive. He followed directions he had picked up in San Francisco, occasionally stopping the car for a visual check of his surroundings . . . and to be certain he wasn't followed. A leisurely forty-minute drive brought him to Bondi Beach. He walked to the pay phone, deposited the coins, and dialed as he had been instructed.

The phone rang inside a fourth-floor apartment. A manicured hand reached for the receiver. "Yes?" a voice said.

"My name is Hollister," the Batman said. "I understand you have been expecting me."

"It might be so," the man in the apartment answered,

his voice as dry and empty as a snake's discarded skin. "Do turn around, if you don't mind."

"Turn around?" the man who said he was Big Jack Hollister asked, feigning confusion.

"Yes. Turn *around*—I'd like to have a look at you," the man in the apartment said, now peering through a telescope trained on the pay phone Hollister was told to use. As Hollister turned, the man in the apartment quickly compared the face with the one in the Polaroid photo he held in his left hand. "That will do," he said, satisfied. "Do you remember what I told you to bring?"

"Yes," Hollister said, holding up a blue gym bag.

"Ah, very good. If you'll just take a little walk . . . say, halfway to the water, and establish yourself, I'll be along directly."

"Okay," Hollister said, but he was speaking into a dead phone.

Hollister found a suitable spot. He opened the gym bag and spread out a khaki army blanket. Then he reached inside the bag and took out a small red cooler in the shape of a tool kit. Satisfied, Big Jack reclined on his back, eyes closed, his face tilted toward the sun as if to take advantage of a tanning opportunity. His highly trained senses combined to inform him of another's approach, but he remained passive until he heard, "Mr. Hollister, I presume?"

Hollister opened his eyes. He was looking up at a portly man dressed in a white suit with matching Panama hat. The man's skin was the color of old copper. He looked as sleek as a seal—his very presence exuded confidence. "Mind if I sit down?" he asked.

Hollister shifted slightly to make room. The portly man opened the red cooler and extracted a bottle of dark East India ale. "You have excellent taste, sir!" he said enthusiastically, removing the bottle cap with a single wrench of his large white teeth.

"I thought we might have some tastes in common," Hollister said.

"Uncommon, more likely, don't you think?" the portly man replied.

"I guess it depends who you ask."

"Yes. Well enough of this silly fencing about, Mr. Hollister. My name is Morad. Now you know all about me that you need to know. Please tell me how I can be of service."

"I am interested in . . . opportunities. In Udon Khai. I have been told you have considerable . . . awareness of conditions there. I was hoping for an introduction, so to speak."

"My dear fellow," Morad spoke. "You are not dealing with that paranoid Drako now—there is no need for all these euphemisms. You wish to enjoy the company of children, yes? Would that be boys or girls?"

"Girls," Hollister said.

"Ah so. For new goods, I mean *truly* new, the price would be . . . oh, roughly ten thousand dollars?"

"Ten grand American? Just for—?"

"Ten grand *Australian*," Morad interrupted. "Perhaps I have not made myself clear. I am talking about a pure virgin, a child no one has *ever* touched. Perhaps, as an American, you fail to appreciate the significance of such an opportunity."

"I understand," Hollister said. "It just seems a bit steep for only one—"

"You need not restrict yourself to a single event," Morad interrupted again. "Although that special moment comes only once, you have the use of the child for twenty-four hours—that is all included in the price, as is an environment suitable to such an accomplishment."

"And this is legal, right? Perfectly legal?"

"Mr. Hollister, legality is a creature of the moment. As we speak, the age of consent in Udon Khai is twelve—sex with a child of at least that age is, in fact, perfectly legal."

"But what if I—?"

"You need go no further," Morad said, again cutting Hollister off in midsentence. "The age of the child is of no consequence to the government in Udon Khai. What *is* affected is the price, do you understand?"

"So for the ten grand . . . ?"

"You get a child not yet twelve. If you require one *much* younger, there would be additional cost considerations."

"It sounds like paradise," Hollister said.

"It *is* paradise," Morad replied. "Even this conversation is completely legal. Even if you were an undercover agent," he began, looking directly into Hollister's eyes, "and even if you were to offer me money and I were to accept it, no crime would have been committed."

"That's amazing."

"Amazing but true, Mr. Hollister. Unfortunately, some antipedophile fascists are trying to change our local laws. If they are successful, it would actually be a felony just to have a conversation such as we are having today. 'Conspiracy,' they would call it. It is an outrageous assault on civil liberties, and I am confident our liberal friends in government will stop it in its tracks. And even were the repressive elements to succeed here, they would find it much tougher sledding in the United States, I can guarantee you that. Politicians in America can always be counted upon to support our causes—America is, in fact, the country with the best understanding of our . . . hobby. There is such hypocrisy in the world! Are *we* not the *true* child advocates? After all, what good is the child's right to say 'No' to sex without the equal right to say 'Yes'?''

Morad mopped his brow with a large black silk handkerchief. Then he drew a deep breath. "But enough of this doom-and-gloom, my friend—we must live in the moment. And for the precious moment you contemplate . . ." He held out a hand, palm up. "Shall we say ten thousand?"

Hollister handed over the money. In return, he received an address in Udon Khai. "Ask for Bhatt Po," Morad told him, "and give him this card."

Hollister took the piece of white pasteboard he was handed. The same size as an ordinary business card, it had a large drawing of a black widow spider on one side, the trademark red-orange hourglass shining on the black sheen of the insect's underbelly. On the other side, Morad had hand-inscribed a series of pictographic characters. "This is all you need," he said.

"Why a black widow?" Hollister asked.

"Why not?" Morad replied. "But, in fact, Mr. Hollister, that is our 'chop' . . . the signature of our organization. It is recognized throughout Udon Khai—if you are there long enough, you will see it many times, in many places."

"I—"

"No thanks are necessary, Mr. Hollister. I am happy to have been of service."

The next night found a tiny jet cruising at forty-five thousand feet, well above any commercial aircraft. At the controls, the Batman checked the coordinates Alfred had beamed to him. He pulled the microphone close to his mouth, then used his right hand to tap in the codes to access the Batcave.

"Yes, sir?" Alfred answered.

"I'm on time," the Batman said. "And on target. If I'm reading these coordinates properly together with the airport schematic, it appears as though I won't be landing on the runway at all. Is that your understanding as well?"

"No sir, it is not. Where you will be landing is an uncharted section of the airport, but it has plenty of runway. When you approach, signal 'Code 33' to the tower. They will *not* acknowledge, but a twin row of landing lights will appear to guide you down."

"And from there?"

"Rhama Bgyn will be waiting, sir. And he will have appropriate transport."

"It sounds as if the airport has done this before."

"All the time," Alfred answered dryly. "It is their assumption that you intend some illicit activity. Perhaps that is why their 'special permit landing fee' was a quarter of a million dollars US, wire-transferred to an account in the Cayman Islands."

"This Rhama Bgyn . . . are you absolutely certain of his credentials?" the Batman asked, not referring to an ability to translate languages.

"His credentials are impeccable, sir," Alfred replied.

"He was thoroughly vetted by our people. In fact, he is wanted by General Ngum's government—a reward has been posted, approximate value in US currency is two thousand dollars—a veritable fortune in that country."

"What is he wanted for?"

"Treason," Alfred said.

The Batman didn't bother to ask if *that* crime carried the death penalty. "Signing off," he said, tilting the nose of the baby jet down to begin the long descent.

As soon as the little jet touched down, it began to merge with the shadows at the end of the outlaw runway, its black-and-gray mottled paint blending perfectly. A slender young man with close-cropped black hair and unreadable eyes emerged from the surrounding underbrush and began to walk slowly toward the jet. There was a faint hiss as the side door opened. A large, powerfully built man climbed down the stairs, carrying a bulky suitcase in his left hand. He marked the approach of the slender young man and walked deliberately toward him at a steady pace. When the two met, the young man extended his hand.

"Rhama Bgyn," he said. "At your service."

"Big Jack Hollister," the other man responded. "Pleased to meet you, pal."

"I regret that the accommodations will be sparse," Rhama Bgyn said to Big Jack as he steered the innocuous sedan gently around a long curve in one of the secondary roads that ringed the capital city. "My . . . employer said you wished privacy above all else, yes?"

"Yes, that's right," Big Jack said. "Don't worry about me—once I get my bearings, I'll be out of your hair."

"Will you not be requiring me for—?"

"There's another man involved," Big Jack said. "He's the one you really have to translate for, okay?"

"I understand."

"But first, I want to kind of have a look around, all right?"

"Yes. Once we are situated, I am at your disposal."

Two nights later, Big Jack Hollister emerged from a night-club. As he paused on the sidewalk, the tawdry neon washed his profile, accentuating a haggard face. It was the fifth club he had visited that night. The fifth club where little girls still years away from becoming teenagers were paraded about on the bar as though they were another offering of food or drink. Choking down a mouthful of bile, Big Jack started a slow trek toward another address he had been given, his eyes rimmed with a red haze that had nothing to do with neon.

The storefront was glass, with ***PHOTOGRAPHS!*** hand-painted in rough script. In the back of the store, Big Jack looked through an album of color pictures. All the photos were of children, boys and girls. None were clothed. Several were engaged in sex acts— with adults, with each other, with animals. The proprietor pointed to each photograph in turn, quoting prices and services in passable English.

The man for whom self-control was the hallmark of his life struggled internally with a secret voice . . . a voice he was hearing for the first time. A voice urging him to violence. Shaking his head as though the movement would rearrange his thoughts, Big Jack Hollister stalked out of the pimp's parlor and back into the street.

"It's time," he muttered to himself.

The Batman traversed the rooftops of Mae Ngao smoothly, marking the location of dead-end streets, one-way alleys, and other strategic locations. He crisscrossed the city, following the information Rhama Bgyn had given to Big Jack, locating several small apartment buildings exclusively used to house sex-industry children. Peering inside, the Batman was overcome with a sadness so profound that his entire body trembled with empathic pain for the captured children.

"Mother, is this the demon you battled?" he asked in his mind.

And across time, across space, across even death, his mother answered.

Rhama Bgyn returned to the shabby house he had rented on the edge of town, expecting to meet the big American journalist. He entered through the front door and carefully made his way to the back of the house where the American slept. The room was empty. Like most people who search a room, Rhama Bgyn never looked up . . . so when the Batman dropped softly to the floor behind him it was as though the night-rider had materialized from nowhere. Startled, Rhama's hand flashed toward his armpit, but the Batman was too quick—the pistol never left its holster.

"Don't be afraid," the Batman said, maintaining his grip on the young man's forearm. "I have not come to hurt you—I have come to ask your help."

"Who are—?"

"Big Jack Hollister must have told you about me," the Batman said softly. "I need a translator."

"Oh. *You* are the one. I did not think . . ."

"That's all right. I need to go to the mountains, and I need a guide."

"The mountains? Outside the city, you mean?"

"Yes. Far outside. I want to go to the places where people sell their children like cattle."

"That is, sadly, a very easy request to meet," Rhama Bgyn said, his eyes still adjusting to the costumed creature who stood before him. "When would you want to go?"

"Now," the Batman said. "Tonight. I need to have a

base established before it gets light. But first, there is another place I want to visit.''

In a narrow alley across from a twisting street, the Batman and his guide watched a dark doorway—the address of Bhatt Po. "Are you able to get inside by showing this card?'' the Batman asked his guide, handing the black widow symbol to him.

"Yes. All the flesh-traders know this chop,'' Rhama said quietly. "It will be unusual for a native to possess one. They would probably ask many questions. But it will certainly get me in the door.''

"Do it,'' the Batman said.

Rhama bowed. When he looked up, he was alone in the alley.

Rhama Bgyn crossed the narrow street furtively, his carriage suggesting some nefarious purpose. A quick series of sharp raps on the wooden door and a narrow panel slid back.

"What is wanted?'' a voice asked in Udon.

Rhama did not answer. Instead, he handed the black widow card through the slot, which immediately closed. A long five minutes passed. The door opened fully. A man dressed in a hooded black *gi* told Rhama to enter, standing aside as he did so. The man in black pointed down a corridor. Rhama walked slowly in that direction, feeling the other man close behind. They entered a long, narrow room where a man of uncertain ancestry sat in a chair that looked as if it had once been a throne. The man in the black *gi* approached, bowed quickly, and handed over the black widow card.

"I am Bhatt Po," the man in the chair spoke. "Where did you get this card?"

"From a man, a white man. He is staying at the hotel. He told me to fetch the girl, and bring her to him."

"That is not permitted," Bhatt Po replied. "It is too dangerous. He must come here."

"Tell him I want the girl," the Batman said, stepping through the door.

Before Rhama could begin the translation, the man in black moved toward the Batman. Up on his toes in a cat-stance, the man in black circled slowly. The Batman stood immobile, as patient as stone. With a sharp cry, the man in black ran forward and leaped into the air, turning at an impossible angle to fire a two-footed strike at the Batman's midsection. The masked man slipped the strike and struck at the exposed inner thigh of his adversary as he flew by. The blow so paralyzed the man in the black *gi* that he could not control his body—his head struck the polished wooden floor with that crackle-crunch sound that always foretells a fractured skull.

"Tell him," the Batman said again, as calm as a man asking for a newspaper.

Rhama spoke in Udon, listening to the response from Bhatt Po, then said, "He says there are no girls here. You have made a mistake. He is very sorry."

"Translate *simultaneously*," the Batman said in a harsh voice. "*Direct.* None of this 'he said, she said,' understand?"

Rhama bowed, waiting.

"Give me the girl. I will not ask again," the Batman said.

"I have no girl here, sir," Rhama said, translating the hurried, frightened speech of Bhatt Po.

"One of two things in this house," the Batman said. "The choice is yours. Either you have the girl, or you have everlasting pain."

"Please, sir. I do not have—"

The Batman strode toward the massive wood desk next to Bhatt Po's throne. His gloved hand flashed. The desk splintered as though it were balsa instead of teak. Bhatt Po's scream was instantly silenced as the Batman grasped his throat. "Your larynx is next," he hissed.

Bhatt Po's face turned a sickly greenish color. His legs trembled uncontrollably. He spoke for almost a minute before he stopped, his hands clasped together in a prayerful gesture.

"Upstairs," was all the translating Rhama needed. The Batman grasped a nerve cluster in Bhatt Po's throat and the merchant collapsed, falling face-forward onto the remains of the smashed desk.

Rhama led the way up a narrow staircase, the Batman right behind. The only light was a fat candle at the end of the hall. In the last room, they found the girl. She looked to be eight or nine years old, dressed in a pure white silk shift, her hair combed until it was glossy. Everything about her was bright and shining except her eyes— they were glazed and vacant.

"She must have fought hard," Rhama said. "They had to drug her."

"Pick her up and follow me," the Batman said.

"Bhatt Po may have more men downstairs," Rhama

warned, hoisting the child onto one shoulder and drawing his automatic with his free hand.

"I hope so," the Batman said, his voice as merciless as a panther's snarl.

"It seems . . . destined," Rhama said to the Batman. They were in Rhama's car, heading out of the city. "You ask to go where the children are sold, and now we are taking one of the children back. I believe it is a sign. But I say to you, with all respect, you should not return this child to her family."

"Why not?"

"Because they *sold* her. They do not admit that, of course. To save face, they always say that the child is going to the city to work, and will send money home. The child buyers, they pay cash. And they say the child must work enough to earn that cash. The child cannot go home until this is done."

"Is it *ever* done?"

"No."

"Perhaps you are right. Let us get into the mountains first, then we will decide."

"As you say, Warrior," Rhama replied, peering through the streaked windshield, eyes alert for government troops. "We will be in the mountains in three hours."

The morning sun broke over the mountain range, slanting across the rocky plateau below, the harsh rays emphasizing the barren ground. The Batman's eyes followed the sun, scanning the arid terrain, watching with the natural patience of the hunter. He was standing just inside the entrance to a cave, as invisible within the shadow as the air itself.

"Warrior, tell me. Will the girl recover?"

The Batman spoke without turning his head, addressing the young man standing just behind him. "Yes. In fact, she would have been alert some time ago—I gave her an additional injection to spread out the wake-cycle—I did not want her to wake up in fear."

"Do you still wish to return her to her family?"

"Yes."

Rhama took a deep breath. He looked at his out-stretched hands, willing them to stop shaking. "Breathe only through your nose," the Batman said quietly, not turning around. "If you breathe through your mouth, you risk hyperventilation. Breathe slowly. Deeply. Take the air all the way in—let it all the way out . . . slowly. Good!"

"How could you know—?" Rhama stopped himself in midsentence. The young man breathed as he had been instructed. He watched in amazement as the tremors left his hands. "Warrior," he asked, "may I speak?"

"Of course."

"I . . . know who you are."

The Batman did not react, having already considered the possibility that the Big Jack Hollister persona would not survive up-close scrutiny.

Encouraged by the silence, Rhama continued: "I call you Warrior because that is the closest translation from our language to English," the young man said. "High in these mountains, deep in a cave, that is where the Warrior lives. All know this. He is called a legend by some. A myth by others. But all know the truth, even if they would deny it."

"I am not—"

"I understand," Rhama interrupted. "I know you must say that. The legend says the Warrior appears in many forms. But when the Warrior appears in the form of a man, all will know. On that day, it is written, the walls will crumble."

"What walls?" the Batman asked, curious in spite of himself.

"The walls that enslave us. We are alone to the world because of the walls. If the walls crack, people will see

inside. And then, there will be the chance—the chance
to fight for our freedom.''

''You sound like a revolutionary,'' the Batman said.

''I hope I do,'' Rhama replied. ''I pray I am. Only a
revolution will save the children of Udon Khai.''

By late afternoon, the little girl was awake and alert. Rhama
gently fed her sips of a clear broth the Batman had brewed,
a special mixture of nutrients designed to quickly convert
to energy under conditions of internal stress. Initially
frightened, the child finally allowed herself to be soothed.
As darkness descended over the mountains, she fell into
a blissfully dreamless sleep.

The Batman and Rhama were on either side of a solar-
powered heating element the Batman had assembled from
his vast store of survival equipment. Easily recharged in
each day's bright sunlight, the heating element produced
no light, but it threw off enough BTUs to warm the entire
cave. The men were seated in the lotus position, each
alone with his thoughts. Finally the Batman spoke: ''When
you spoke of walls . . . walls that enslave your people, there
was an air of bitterness in your voice that seemed directed
at the outside world. Is that true?''

''Yes, Warrior. That is true. It is both terrible and
true.''

''Will you explain?''

''The children of this country, where are their advocates? Where are all the people outraged around the
world? There are many myths that leave evil in their wake,
is that not so?''

"It is so."

"Yes. There is a myth that a powder made from the horn of a rhino is an aphrodisiac. That myth is under a powerful attack. Environmentalists all over the world want to save the rhino, so they make it illegal to traffic in rhino horn, they shoot poachers on sight, and they have a huge media campaign to explain that the rhino horn does not help a man with his . . . potency. This does not stop all of it, but it stops a great deal."

"Why does that disturb you?" the Batman asked.

"There are other myths," the young man said, his simmering anger barely under control. "A myth that sex with a little girl will restore sexual prowess. A myth that sex with a little boy is safe, because you cannot get AIDS from a child."

"But those myths are not—"

"Not what, Warrior? Not *true*? What is true is what people believe. Where is the public relations campaign to attack *those* myths? Where are the laws that protect the children? Why should it be that men of evil can plot to come here and rape our children and that this is not a crime in their home country? Where are the boycotts, the blockades, the economic sanctions? When will we shoot the poachers of *children* on sight?"

"How did you come to these beliefs?" the Batman asked. "Were you a private investigator?" Like my mother was, he thought.

"A *private* investigator? We have no such word in our language, Warrior. The only investigators here are from the army. And all they investigate are the rebels, not those who sell children. You wish to know how I learned this? I will tell you," he said, dropping the volume of his voice even as its intensity increased. "I am the son of a doctor.

I had all the advantages: a fine education, servants in the house, even a car when I was only fourteen. My life was bliss, because I was blind.

"My mother's family was from the mountains. Sometimes my parents would drive out there to see them. My father would distribute little gifts, like a king handing out alms. It always embarrassed me, but I still liked to go with them.

"I had a little cousin," Rhama Bgyn continued. "Lily was her name. She was a beautiful child. I was only a few years older than her, but I felt as though I was her big brother. I always protected her." The young man took a breath. Then he bit sharply into his lower lip, trying to bite back the tears. "They took her, Warrior. They came to her village in the mountains and they took her.

"When we went to visit, Lily's father said she went to the city to live with other relatives, but he lied. I looked everywhere. My father forbade my search, but I continued anyway. And I found my little Lily, Warrior. By the time I found her, she had become one of *Les Enfants du Secret*."

"Children of the Secret? I don't—"

"The secret is our shame, Warrior. The shame of our nation, and the shame of all the other nations that send their men to use our babies. Lily was a . . . toy. She was used, the first time for much money, and after that, for less and less money all the time. Finally, she was being used in a filthy little shack, many times a night, over and over. When I finally found her, she did not recognize me. But when we talked, she knew I had come for her." The young man drew another harsh breath, willing himself to finish his painful tale of truth. "I had pretended I was a . . . customer, but I knew I would need weapons to rescue Lily. Guns are easy to buy anywhere in Udon Khai, but they are expensive. I could not ask my father—he had disowned me for disobedience when I would not stop searching for Lily. I was surviving only by stealing. I knew it would take many years to save the money for a gun, so I did what was necessary. I went into the mountains. The rebels captured me. I told them what I wanted. I traded my soul for two pistols. I found my Lily in the same place. I went inside, back to the big room that was separated into cubicles by blankets dropped from the ceiling. I gave one pistol to Lily. We walked softly, but we knew we would be discovered. Lily shot the man at the front of the place where they used her. We made it out into the street, but then the soldiers came. I was hit twice. Lily died there. Died in the street. But I know her soul was at peace.''

''How did you get away?'' the Batman asked.

''I did not get away, Warrior. When my wounds healed, I was put into Ghajhat Prison. My own father renounced me. I was found guilty of treason. Yes, in Udon Khai, it is treason to rescue one of *Les Enfants du Secret*. I was to be executed, but I had to wait—there were so many others ahead of me for the hangman's rope. One night, there was an enormous explosion—the rebels had dynamited the side of the prison to free some of their comrades. Many of us escaped. Many of us did not. The government held mass executions after that.''

''When you say you sold your soul . . . ?''

''To the rebels, Warrior. I knew nothing of politics then. I agreed to fight on their side until they achieved victory or until I died. But it would not have mattered. Once I understood how my Lily was used, I knew I could never rest until she was avenged. I am a rebel, too,'' the young man said, eyes shining through a veneer of tears.

"Not some 'outside agitator,' not some 'Communist' . . . a rebel against the tyranny that feeds our babies to beasts."

The Batman said nothing for a long minute. Then he extended one gloved hand. Rhama Bgyn grasped the offered hand and felt its power . . . felt the power flow into him.

"Tomorrow," the Batman said. "It begins."

At dawn the next day, a villager spotted a strange trio descending from the mountains. First came a slender young man carrying a rifle. Behind him was a little girl, dressed all in white. And last was a shadowy figure that resembled nothing so much as a huge bat . . . a huge bat *walking*. The villager ran to report the news.

By the time the trio entered the packed-earth circle that served as a village square, every eye was on them.

"Remember," the Batman said to Rhama, "*simultaneous* translation."

"Yes, Warrior," the young man said. He cleared his throat, then commanded the father of the little girl to come forward. A man stumbled toward the trio. He was in his mid-thirties, but his back was bowed and many of his teeth were missing. His posture was that of a fawning, subservient lackey. His fear was palpable.

Rhama Bgyn pointed at the Batman, listened to his whispered words, then spoke them aloud in a clear, powerful voice.

"Is this your child?" to the man standing before them.

"Yes."

"You sold this child?"

"Not . . . sold," the man stammered. "She would be back when she earned enough money."

"Do not dare to lie! How much money were you paid?"

"Three hundred thousand klong."

Some of the villagers gasped in disbelief—a sum so large could never be repaid in anyone's lifetime.

"Do you want your daughter back?" the Batman asked through Rhama's words.

"A bargain is a bargain," the father said. "I cannot return the money, so . . ."

"What kind of a man would sell his child into slavery?"

The father kept his head bowed, not answering. The Batman's eyes swept around the circle of villagers, challenging each in turn. Finally another man stepped forward. "May I speak?" he asked.

"Yes."

"We know who you are, Warrior. And we know you have come for a reason. That reason is not known to us, but perhaps your question is the answer."

"Speak plainly!"

"Very well. I am the leader here. I know this place well. I was born here. I will die here. This man," he said, indicating the father who still stood with his head bowed, "had nine children. *Nine.* How could they be fed? The ground is as hard as General Ngum's heart. The poppy does not grow well in this part of the country. Only a few goats can live at the same time on the foraging we have available. He knows it is wrong to sell a child. His heart is heavy with pain. But I ask you, Warrior, with all respect, if you were this poor father, what would *you* do?''

The Batman stood silent, feeling the words more than hearing them. The villagers fell silent as well, waiting for the answer to a question as old as evil itself. The Batman flashed back to the alley where his parents had been murdered. To his life since that night. To the dedication of that life to fighting crime. He faced the villagers, speaking in a slow, deliberate voice as Rhama translated:

"I would not feed my children with the blood of one of their sisters or brothers. If I were to stand where you have stood, I would steal.''

A hush fell over the village. Then the leader spoke up. "Warrior, out here, there is nothing to steal. There is no money here. What would you have us do then?''

"Those who buy your children have money,'' the Batman said. "And you know where to find them.''

By nightfall, the trio was deep into the mountains. The little girl had fallen asleep, her arms wrapped around the Batman's neck. He cradled the child easily with one hand, walking catfooted over the broken terrain.

After another hour, Rhama Bgyn halted. "We are close now, Warrior. I cannot know how my people will react when I speak to them. It would be a tragedy if they were to attack you, for I know you cannot be defeated. It is better that you follow me in the sky. If they agree to help, you will know. If not, you must return to the city. I will try and get back there as soon as possible."

"Thank you," the Batman said.

"It is my honor," the young man replied.

The Batman handed the sleeping child to Rhama Bgyn. Then he turned with a swirl of his cape and melted into the night.

Rhama Bgyn gently roused the little girl. "Wake up, little sister," he said. "We have to walk now. Not too far, all right?" Rhama Bgyn gently picked up the child, held her for a moment, then put her on her feet.

The little girl looked up at Rhama Bgyn, her dark eyes as deep and luminescent as a mountain pool. She bowed slightly, then held out her hand. Rhama Bgyn accepted the child's hand as he would a sacred trust. Together, they started to walk.

It was another quarter mile before a sentry stepped from behind a rock, an ancient Chinese version of the infamous AK-47 in his hand.

"Oh, Rhama Bgyn," he said. "You have been gone a long while. Who is this?"

"This is my sister," the young man replied. "Her name is Lily."

The sentry waved the two travelers on, returning to his post. As he placed his rifle on the ground, the Batman withdrew from his hiding place and continued to follow.

The two travelers kept walking until they reached the rebel camp. After an exchange of greetings, they were taken to a large campfire around which guerillas, both men and women, sat. Rhama Bgyn kept his feet, speaking in a voice firm with conviction. Atop a craggy outcropping thirty feet up from the ground, the Batman watched. He could not follow the rapid conversation, but it was clearly some form of argument. The words grew increasingly shrill. A young woman dressed in army fatigues rose to her feet, slowly and deliberately. She crossed the clearing to stand beside Rhama Bgyn. In her right hand, she held a pistol—her left hand was on the shoulder of the child Rhama had named Lily.

The arguments continued. Escalated. More of the rebels walked over to stand with Rhama Bgyn, but the majority held their positions on the ground. Finally Rhama Bgyn opened both arms, as though appealing to the heavens. "Warrior!" he called out. "Warrior, now is the time. You are needed!"

The guerillas stared in puzzlement, wondering why their comrade was speaking in such a strange tongue. Perhaps that is why they were so startled when the Batman dropped out of the night sky to stand before them. With his cape fully extended, the Batman looked several times the size of any man. The rebels froze in their places, spellbound at the appearance of the spirit.

"Some wish to attack the castle," Rhama Bgyn said quietly. "They stand with us. Others wish to continue as we have . . . as guerilla fighters."

"What is the castle?" the Batman asked.

"It is the den of the demon—and this is his chop," Rhama Bgyn replied, handing over the white card with the black widow spider symbol. "He is protected by the army. Now that the opium business is so difficult, it is *his* business . . . the slavery of children . . . that brings General

Ngum the foreign exchange. If we stop him, the government cannot survive.''

"You must—" the Batman began to speak. One of
the guerillas leaped to his feet, drew a pistol from his
holster, and fired directly at the Batman's chest. The Batman's body armor absorbed most of the shock—his
trained body did the rest. He immediately waved his hands
for silence—a gesture rendered unnecessary by the open-
mouthed shock on the faces of the guerillas. The man
who had fired the shot looked at his pistol suspiciously,
then quickly reholstered it, looking in every direction but
toward the Batman.

"This is the Warrior!" Rhama Bgyn proclaimed. "He
has come! With my own eyes, I saw him defeat one of
Bhatt Po's ninjas as though the ninja were an infant. You
cannot harm him with your guns. And he will not harm
us. He is *with* us, my brothers and sisters. Let him speak,
now!''

The Batman stood as implacably as the surrounding
mountains. His speech was so smoothly translated by
Rhama Bgyn that it seemed to the guerillas that he was
speaking in their tongue. "To sell a child is a violation of
all humanity," the Batman said. "Even the lowest animal
will die to protect its child. Can we call ourselves a higher
form when we fail to do the same? To sell children for
the pleasure and profit of others is a mortal sin. It is the
ultimate evil. And it is time for the evil to end!''

"What shall we do, Warrior?" one of the guerillas
asked, rapidly translated by Rhama Bgyn.

"Can you take the castle?" the Batman asked in
return.

"Yes," another guerilla answered. "It is guarded, but

not so well. We will lose some of our people. But we could take it. The question is . . . could we hold it?''

The Batman fixed his gaze upon the speaker.

"You do not *need* to hold it," he said. "The child-sex syndicate is a monolith." The Warrior spoke, making a pyramid of his fingers and thumbs to illustrate. "Once the head is gone, the body will die."

"Others could take his place," a woman said.

"Yes," the Batman replied. "But it will take time for that to happen. Time for you to consolidate your positions against General Ngum. Time for the general to flee to Paraguay or Saudi Arabia or some other hospitable country. Time for the army to defect. Their soldiers are not patriots, they are mercenaries—their loyalty is only as strong as their paycheck."

"The Warrior speaks the truth!" the woman who had been the first to stand with Rhama Bgyn proclaimed. "How many more must be lost to the evil of *Les Enfants du Secret?*"

"Think of the risk, Opal," one of the young men admonished her. "We are of no use to the revolution dead."

"I joined the movement to die," the woman named Opal snapped back. "To *die* honorably so that those who follow me can *live* honorably. What good is your life? A man who does nothing *is* nothing!"

Sporadic arguments broke out all along the perimeter of the campfire. Rhama Bgyn stood by in silence, holding the hand of the newly named Lily, waiting with the patience of a much older man.

The Batman stood immobile.

Even the child maintained an eerie silence.

The force of the Batman's will radiated out from the center of his soul. Joined in progress by the merging spirits of Rhama Bgyn and the girl-child he now adored as he had his beloved Lily, swelling with the heart of the young woman called Opal, the spiritual force was so palpable that several of the guerillas began to weep, crying for the lost souls of Udon Khai's children.

"We are with you, Warrior!" Rhama Bgyn spoke for them all. "We will need a week and three days to prepare. Ten days from midnight, we will storm the castle of the demon."

The Batman bowed deeply. "I will be with you," Rhama translated. "From now until then."

The caped figure backed away from the campfire, never looking behind him. In less than a minute, he was gone.

Four days later, a refrigerator-white Land Rover slowly picked its way along a rocky mountain path. The four-wheel-drive vehicle's heavy-duty suspension and huge off-road tires were sorely tested by the broken terrain, but the driver was a veteran of many such passages. As the vehicle rounded a particularly sharp hairpin turn, two of the guerillas stepped out from cover, their rifles trained on the lone driver.

"Step down! Now!" one of the guerillas barked.

The driver climbed out. The guerillas noted he was European, a chubby middle-aged man with streaks of gray in his longish hair. "I was wondering if I would *ever* find you," he said in perfect Udon, his face illuminated by a sunny smile. "I have a gift—a gift for Lily Bgyn."

"What is this gift?" the guerilla spokesman demanded.

"See for yourself," the driver said, standing aside.

The guerillas opened the rear hatch of the Land Rover. It was packed with neat wooden cases. "Go fetch Rhama," the guerilla who did all the talking told the other. "I will stay here to watch this smiling dog."

Ninety minutes later, Rhama Bgyn walked up to the Land Rover and looked inside. "Do you know what is in here?" he asked the driver.

"Sure," the driver said, still smiling. "The question is: do *you* know?" Ignoring the rifle pointed at his back, the driver reached into the back of the Land Rover and pulled out a metal tube about two feet long. "Watch carefully," he said. The driver pulled on one end of the tube, which popped out to almost twice the original length. "That arms it," he said. "Now, you see this?" he asked, pointing with a finger from which the tip was missing. "This is the sight—it pops up when you pull on one end, like I just did."

"What is it?" Rhama Bgyn asked, intrigued in spite of himself.

"This is an LAAW," the driver said. "Light Anti-Armor Weapon. It fires a rocket that will penetrate a solid foot of steel. Weighs about ten pounds. Has almost *no* recoil—anyone can use one."

"What do you load it with?" Rhama Bgyn asked.

"It *is* loaded," the driver replied. "When you open it up, that arms the rocket inside. You can't reload it—you blast it off, then you throw it away. You use it, you lose it, understand? You got an even dozen of them in there," he said, gesturing at the Land Rover. "Now, once you get the walls down, you'll need some suppressive fire—

to keep the enemy's heads down, right? Okay, that beast on the tripod in there? That's a fifty-caliber machine gun. Plus there's a pair of M-60s, thirty-caliber, faster than you can count: zip, zip, zip—that'll keep their heads down for sure."

"What makes you think—?"

"Let me finish, my young friend," the driver said. "You also have eight boxes of concussion grenades, one box of flash-bangs. Over in the far corner, that long tubed thing? That's a flamethrower."

"Have you brought any rifles?" Rhama Bgyn asked.

"I understand the objective is stone, yes?" the driver replied. "Inside such a structure, ricochet is a big problem. So we got you ten street-sweepers: twelve-gauge short-stroke pump shotguns, capacity's an even dozen rounds. The shells are three-inch Magnums, but the double-O buck has been replaced with very soft lead. If you hit someone, they're gone. But if you miss, the soft lead will just splatter against the wall, not bounce around."

"Is that all?" Rhama Bgyn asked, a trace of sarcasm in his voice.

"No. I also have some battlefield first-aid kits, including morphine and penicillin. There is also—"

"That is enough!" Rhama commanded. "Who sent you?"

"He never mentioned his name," the driver said with a smile. "All I know is he was American. Like me."

"What did the white man look like?"

"He was very big, heavyset. His hair was pulled straight back, very greasy. He had an ugly scar, right here . . ." the driver said, his forefinger tracing a jagged line on his right temple.

"Big Jack Hollister," Rhama Bgyn said to himself. "What were your instructions?" he said aloud.

"I was to follow the route he gave me. When I was stopped, I was to say all the weapons are a gift. A gift for Lily Bgyn."

"The gift is from the Warrior," Rhama said to Opal. "He works through others, but it is *his* work. Already he is clearing our path to the demon."

Two nights later, a low-flying jet swooped down on the guerilla camp so quickly that only the sonic boom indicated its passage. Then a bundle attached to a Day-Glo orange parachute slowly dropped to earth, visible even at night. Where the bundle touched earth, a cold green fire formed a visible aura—the searchers had no trouble locating it.

Opened, the bundle contained a fortune in Udon Khai klongs.

"It is a test," Rhama Bgyn said to the guerilla band. "A test for all of us—the test of a warrior."

The bundle of money was brought back to camp and left standing in the open all night.

At daylight, the money remained untouched.

"That is enough to insure the silence of many, many houses along the way to the castle," Opal said, pointing to the bundle. "If a man will take money to overlook evil, he will take money to overlook those who stalk it."

The moon shone full, bathing the land in cold, pale light. As the Batman watched from his perch, he could see the guerilla units quietly deploying, readying the assault. The "castle" was, in fact, a magnificent house built from native stone right into the side of a mountain, so skillfully integrated that it appeared to be a natural out-cropping. The night-rider's trained eyes picked out several guard posts—but he assumed the real defensive strength was inside the house itself.

As the moon dropped behind a cloud, the Batman started his ascent.

When he reached a purchase above the first guard post, the Batman pulled a six-inch tube from inside his cape. A flick of his wrist and the tube extended to three feet. His practiced fingers working effortlessly in the dark, the Batman fitted a needle-tipped dart into the tube, then put one end in his mouth. The night-rider's chest swelled to seemingly impossible proportions. He held his breath as he focused on his target—the exposed neck of the sentry. The Batman expelled his breath in one massive jolt. The dart zipped into the guard's neck. The nerve poison worked instantly. The guard crumpled to the ground.

Three sentries later—three sentries who would, if they were lucky, remain unconscious throughout the assault— the Batman was inside the house. He prowled the high ceilings, sensors on full alert. As he peered down into a large barracks-style room where dozens of men lounged about, a red light began to flash as a warning siren blared— the assault was on!

Ignoring the onrushing soldiers, the Batman began to work his way toward the highest point in the house, some instinct telling him that his target would be there. He swung down from his perch and started up a narrow stairway. A tiny rearrangement of the shadows ahead warned him—he backflipped off the stairs just as a soldier fired a burst from an Uzi, stitching a row of bullet holes all along the wall. The Batman astonished the soldier by charging *up* the stairs—before the soldier could recover, he was tumbling down those same stairs, headfirst.

At the top of the stairs a man in a red kimono stood quietly, radiating inner calm, a bamboo stave in his two hands. As the Batman approached, the kendo master began to twirl the stave, his bare feet noiseless as he moved into an attack position. The Batman locked eyes with his adversary and closed the space between them. The kendo master swept his stave from lower right to upper left, then suddenly stopped in midstrike and reversed his hands, his powerful wrists driving the stave at the Batman's exposed neck, but the Batman whirled inside the arc and drove a spinning back-fist into the other man's chest. Before the kendo master could recover, the Batman grabbed his opponent's ears and delivered a vicious head-butt. The kendo master collapsed like a punctured balloon.

As the sounds of gunfire grew more audible behind him, the Batman continued to climb. On the final landing he heard the staccato clicking of claws on marble—some large animal, struggling for a purchase on the slick under-footing. As the Batman cautiously peered around the corner, he saw a magnificent snow leopard barely held in check by a chain around its neck. A muscular woman in a black Mohawk haircut held the chain. When she saw the Batman, she dropped the chain, screaming "Kill, Chui! Kill!" The beast leaped toward the Batman, who turned sideways and took the charge on his right forearm, spinning with the beast's momentum and flinging his arm like a whip to add to it. The leopard shot down the marble hall, vainly trying to stop its slide. It bounced off the far wall, dazed. The beast shook itself and turned its feline eyes back in the direction from which it had come. The muscular woman was crouched, poised with a glistening throwing knife in her right hand. The Batman was still in motion, sliding toward her on the marble floor. The woman threw the knife, but the sliding man slapped it out of the air and continued his slide, kicking the woman's legs out from under her. She fell into the Batman's embrace—an embrace that took her consciousness within seconds.

The sounds of small-arms fire filled the stone house. From outside, there was an occasional *whooomp!* as the rocket launchers did their work. The leopard quickly scanned the scene, as though making up its mind. Then it turned and cat-footed its way down the stairs, profoundly uninterested in humans and their insanity.

The Batman spotted the door from which the woman and the leopard had emerged. It fit so seamlessly that it would have been undetectable by the human eye had it been fully closed. Slowly the night-rider eased the door open. Inside was darkness, a darkness so silent that the air itself seemed audible. The Batman drew a deep yoga breath to center himself, his hunter's instinct telling him that impatience could rob him of his quarry. When the night-rider's heartbeat and pulse had slowed sufficiently, he closed his eyes to avoid sudden night blindness and moved ahead, now a part of the darkness itself.

Less than ten steps into the darkness, the Batman's sonar bounced back the impression of a tunnel. Cautiously he reached out with a gloved hand. The surrounding material felt rough to the touch. Was it concrete? No—the texture was all wrong. The Batman stood quietly, breathing deeply through his nose, focusing all his senses on the material. It smelled like . . . yes! . . . a thick layer of cork. No wonder the place was so silent. Maintaining contact with the cork wall with his right hand, the Batman moved down the tunnel, his left hand extended, moving with the deceptively delicate gait of the true *karateka*.

Forty careful paces into the cork tunnel and the Batman saw a slanted sliver of light ahead—a corner of some kind. As he neared the light, the Batman felt a radical shift in temperature—the air ahead was hot and moist. The Batman slowly removed his right hand from the cork wall and switched to a ninja gait known as crane-walking, moving ahead with the toes of his left foot, all his weight on the back foot. He brought the left foot down toes first, as though carefully descending into water, then dragged his right until the feet touched, switching so smoothly that the right foot became the leader. This allowed him to scan both left and right walls while still minimizing his silhouette.

As the night-rider moved forward, his senses became even more attuned to his surroundings. The slanted sliver of light grew closer, washing the walls with a dull illumination of diffused orange. The silence was broken by tiny sounds: the rustle of paper, the hum of computer terminals, the . . . the Batman's gloved hand shot out, snatching the striking snake just behind its head. The snake hissed in rage, squirming in the night-rider's grip, but the Batman held it at arm's length as he moved toward the light.

The Batman peered around the corner where the light was coming from, the snake still in his right hand. He found himself on a catwalk, the metal railings barely visible. In the faint light the Batman was able to determine that the snake was a greenish-yellow color, banded with another, darker shade of green. The night-rider had never seen such a snake, but one glance at its triangular head told him all he needed to know—it was some form of pit viper, obviously planted as an emergency sentry. That explained the heat and humidity change—snakes cannot remain active in the cold.

The Batman followed the catwalk until he came to another corner. Below was a circle of focused white light. In the circle was a man—an elderly man who sat calmly smoking a pipe as if gunfire and explosions were everyday fare.

To the man's right stood a state-of-the-art telex, a fax machine, and three computer monitors, all linked by cables to an industrial-size laser printer. To the man's left was a giant globe on which a map of the world had been painted. The man held a telephone in his left hand. He was speaking calmly, but in the voice of one who is accustomed to instant obedience.

"It appears we are having some difficulty here," he said. "Nothing we cannot handle, I am sure. It will take hours for the rebels to get in here—the only door visible to invaders is several inches of heavy-gauge steel. Nevertheless, it might be prudent if my allotment of troops could be increased . . . say *within the next ten minutes, damn it!*"

The man slammed down the telephone receiver. Then he appeared to recover his composure and took another soothing puff on his pipe. The distinctive smell of opium wafted up to where the Batman lurked.

William X. Malady, the kingpin of the organization that took his parents' life—he could be no other. The Batman's chest tightened. His fists clenched involuntarily—only the faint sound of cracking bones alerted him. He looked at his right hand, now holding a dead snake.

The night-rider dropped the snake to the floor of the catwalk and gathered himself for the final leap. But before he could act, the heavy steel doors at one end of the large room blew off their hinges. The seated man was frantically rooting around in a desk drawer when Rhama Bgyn entered, a pistol in his hand.

"Put your hands where I can see them," he said in English.

The seated man complied, once again apparently calm. "Do I know you?" he asked.

"My name would mean nothing to you," Rhama Bgyn replied. "Nor would the names of any of the children you stole."

"I am sure you don't—"

"Be sure of nothing but your death if you make a wrong move," Rhama interrupted. "Your day is done now, William Malady. Your soldiers are gone. Only a few died— the rest ran like the cowards they are. What I want from you is your list."

"My list?"

"*Les Enfants du Secret,*" Rhama said, his voice as stony as the house he had invaded. "I need to know where they are, where the children are."

"My dear fellow," Malady said, "you cannot seriously expect me to have such information. You are aware of how it works, I know. The children are sold—"

"The stake is your life," Rhama Bgyn said calmly. "If you have nothing to play with, so be it."

The Batman watched, frozen on his perch, as the seated man spread his hands wide and spoke. "You cannot alter the course of events, my young friend. You have seen my chop. Do you think you understand it?"

"The black widow spider? Yes, I understand it. The spider is poison. And so are you."

"No, you do *not* understand," the seated man said, his voice silky with confidence. "The spider is of no conse- quence—the true meaning is in the hourglass. Look closely. You have climbed a mountain, but you have only come to the middle of the hourglass. Do you understand? You can kill me, but you will have achieved nothing! Noth- ing at all. As long as there are those who sell their children, there are those who will buy. You are not at the top of a peak, you are at the base of a *new* mountain, one with even steeper slopes. Things have changed, but human nature has not. Don't you understand? This is a *business*, that's all."

"The business of evil."

"Whatever you say," Malady replied. "Words change nothing. I will tell you what *does* change things . . . technology changes things. When I began in this business, it was necessary to have . . . associates in order to produce the product. One needed film processors willing to look the other way, distribution was so very difficult, the product itself was of low quality and could not be easily reproduced. Today, that has all changed. Any adult who owns a child . . . a parent or, for that matter, anyone to whom a parent entrusts their child . . . anyone can make a perfectly commercial video in the privacy of their own home. What you would call 'child pornography' is a cottage industry now. The networks are all gone. I am an anachronism. A relic. To kill me would change nothing."

"You stole my Lily!" Rhama Bgyn said, his voice thick with pain.

"If it were not me, it would only be someone else," William Malady said, his smile hideous with self-confidence. "I understand you feel wronged. And I am completely open to the concept of reparations. I'm sure we can work something out. Believe me, my heart is heavy with the pain of—"

"You have no heart," Rhama Bgyn said, his pistol as steady as his words. "You are not a man, you are a peddler of children."

The Batman focused in on the face of Rhama Bgyn, preparing to leap. Suddenly he froze, standing stock-still, his eyes riveted on Malady's left foot . . . a foot gently tapping as though keeping time to music . . . a foot only inches away from a button set into the floor. Even as the Batman reached toward his utility belt, Malady's foot pressed down on the button. The flesh peddler leaned back in his leather chair, a relaxed smile spreading across his face.

"My young friend, I understand your anger. Believe me, I do. If you will give me two minutes . . . literally two minutes—see that clock on the wall—I promise you I will change your mind. Give me two minutes, and after that . . ." Malady shrugged his shoulders, eloquently placing his life in the hands of another.

"Speak," Rhama Bgyn said. "And speak the truth or they will be your last words."

"Very well," Malady began, but the Batman was no longer listening—every one of his senses was tuned to the last sound he heard . . . the unmistakable sound of a round being chambered in a bolt-action rifle. The night-rider leaped lightly onto the railing of the catwalk, balancing as easily as a pedestrian on pavement. Slowly he began to move in the direction of the sound, his eyes boring into the murky shadows.

Another four steps and the Batman's night vision picked up a glint of light. He slowed his breathing again, concentrating. There it was!—a sniper rifle, complete with telescopic sight, poised atop a tripod for better accuracy. As Malady's voice droned on below, the Batman bent at the waist and made a quick movement with his hands. Then he stepped back a dozen paces and dove off the catwalk, disappearing at the end of the Batrope he had lashed in place.

The rifleman was peering through his scope, setting the crosshairs to rest precisely on Rhama Bgyn's chest. He smiled to himself, knowing he had almost another full minute before his employer's time was up. Suddenly the scope's image went black as the Batman flowed over the railing from the darkness below. The rifleman was a killer, not a fighter—

his mouth was still open in amazement when the Batman's fist took him right below the ear at the hinge of the jaw.

The Batman turned his back on the unconscious rifleman and peered down. "Now I must stop Rhama Bgyn," he commanded himself. But he could not will his body to move. He watched the two men beneath him, frozen in time as the young guerilla spoke.

"You have had your two minutes, liar," Rhama Bgyn said.

"Please . . ." Malady whined, fighting to remain calm, knowing his rifleman had failed but not knowing why. "Whatever one man steals, another man can return," the flesh peddler offered, down to his last card—the one card that had always worked for him. "Restitution can always be made—"

"What you steal can never be returned," Rhama Bgyn said, his voice a blend of all emotions. "You stole my Lily— you steal childhood itself!"

The Batman's body went rigid as unchecked emotions exploded within him. *You steal childhood itself!* The horror of that reality resonated within him, acid on the glass surface of his soul, forever etching a deep pattern of pain. His spirit trembled before the onslaught, vibrating at the perfect pitch to shatter the delicate crystal of a child's heart. The night-rider staggered with the pain, clenching his eyes shut, shivering, nearly lost. For several horrifying seconds, the child within the Batman writhed in fear. Terrified, he called his mother's name. And when she answered, the warrior emerged. With a last deep shudder, the night-rider left his past and turned to face his future.

Down below, Rhama Bgyn raised the pistol, his face a mask of anguish. The Batman saw the young man's finger whiten on the trigger. He gathered himself, preparing to leap, but invisible hands held him at bay. He could only watch as . . .

"You took my Lily . . . and now there is a new Lily," Rhama Bgyn intoned, his voice deep with finality. "It may be true, what you say. Someone else may follow. But you, monster, you will steal childhood no more!" Rhama Bgyn cried out as his pistol fired its message. William X. Malady spilled backward off his chair, dead before he hit the floor.

The young man walked over to the body of the man who stole children. Another guerilla came through the door. It was Opal, a rifle in one hand.

"It is done, Rhama," she said. "We must go—the soldiers will be here soon."

"What of the Warrior?" the young man asked, still looking down at Malady.

As the Batman followed Rhama's gaze, Opal said, "The Warrior walks where he will, Rhama. We must go back now."

Rhama stood, seemingly rooted to the spot, still looking down at the dead man.

"Lily needs us," Opal said quietly.

Slowly, Rhama nodded. He looked toward the heavens . . . and saw the Batman looking down. The Batman bowed. Rhama bowed in return.

Rhama and Opal walked together out of the demon's den.

And the Batman, alone with the dead man's computer network, sat down to complete the destruction of his foul empire.

Three weeks later, Alfred brought a carafe of water and some wheat biscuits down to the cave on a silver tray. "I have more news to report," he said, placing the tray next to the Batman.

"From Udon Khai?"

"Yes. The revolution continues to gather strength. What started with sporadic raids on centers of child prostitution has escalated dramatically. It appears as though the rebels have been joined by some of the mountain tribespeople, an utterly unexpected development. Many of the regular army soldiers have deserted, and General Ngum has fled the country. Our sources indicate that he traveled south through Thailand and left the area in an oceangoing yacht named the *Lollypop*."

"Have they been spotted—?"

"The *Lollypop* was blown apart somewhere in the Indian Ocean, Master Bruce. A Greek tanker was close enough to see it all. The captain of that ship reports that there were no survivors—the explosion literally blew the *Lollypop* into bits."

"Is Udon Khai stable yet?"

"No, Master Bruce. Although the rebels control the mountains, pitched battles continue in the streets. But the sex tourism business is dead—as dead as its kingpin."

"William X. Malady."

"Yes. I understand how you feel about it, Master Bruce, but—"

"I could have stopped it, Alfred. I *knew* what Rhama was going to do. I could have stopped it."

"No, Master Bruce. You could not have stopped it . . . or you would have. Accept it."

"Alfred, I . . ." Bruce Wayne started crying softly. His faithful friend walked over to him and put a hand on his shoulder. "The sex tourism business has been smashed," he said. "Your mother is proud of you."

"You mean she *would* be—"

"I mean precisely what I said," Alfred said. "Fighting evil is the same as fighting crime, only the focus is more concentrated. As you have often said, you swim toward the horizon. You will never reach the goal your*self*, but that is of no importance. As you follow your mother's work, others will follow you. It is the soul of the true warrior to struggle so that others can claim the prize."

Then the faithful Alfred walked away, leaving the Batman to his thoughts.

Midnight in Gotham. A bat-shaped shadow soared high, the better to observe the depths below. The night-rider looked with new eyes, the meaning of the black widow's hourglass now engraved on his soul.

From above, the city's underbelly was clearly visible. A teenage girl took a last hit off a crack pipe, desperately seeking an anesthetic before she went back to selling pieces of herself to the anonymous men who cruised by in their expensive cars. In a nearby alley, her spiritual brother lurked, a lead pipe in his hand, telling himself he committed nightly acts of violence to get money but, inside himself, knowing the ugly truth.

Across town, in a luxurious brownstone, a boy who had dropped out of a prestigious prep school revised a suicide note on his home computer, a good-bye letter to the preacher who had taught him hypocrisy. In a nearby high-rise building, his soul sister looked down from the top floor, pregnant with her father's child, praying she would soon be as dead as her dreams.

As he swung from one building to another, the Batman spoke across time. "I understand now, Mother. The Children of the Secret are here, too. They are everywhere." The night-rider swept the scene below him with his eyes, zeroing in. He looked at the patchwork of lights that ranged from candlepoints to neon. "They are all connected by a common evil," he thought. "And someday, they will join together in a force powerful enough to shake this universe. Until then . . ."

Landing lightly on his feet outside a window, the

Batman heard the child's sobbing protest, the guttural grunt of an adult. The information Debra Kane had given him was, as always, accurate.

He looked inside. Saw the video camera poised on a tripod. "In their name!" the Batman cried deep within himself as he swung through the open window to face the ultimate evil.

*The Batman
is a Myth
The Ultimate Evil
is not.
The Truth follows . . .*

Child Sex Tourism

by David Hechler

Child sex tourism is not new. For years pedophiles[1] seeking to avoid severe punishment in the United States have taken trips to countries where prostituted children are plentiful and sexual abuse laws are lenient, unenforced, or (with the help of a bribe or two) easily circumvented.

The subject crops up regularly in pedophile newsletters. One article that appeared in the *NAMBLA Bulletin,* the newsletter of the North American Man/Boy Love Association,[2] rhapsodized about a twelve-year-old Asian boy who, the anonymous author assured readers, "truly loved his work." The writer went on to advise:

> Weigh the pros and cons of becoming involved yourself in sex tourism overseas. Seek and find love from American boys on a platonic, purely emotional level. For sexual satisfaction, travel once or twice yearly overseas. You might get arrested overseas for patronizing a boy prostitute. But the legal consequences of being caught patronizing a boy prostitute in a friendly place overseas will be less severe.[3]

There is evidence that many have heeded this advice:

- A pedophile was advised by friends to go to Asia, where "thousands of kids were there just for the picking." He attended a NAMBLA meeting and afterward confided to a member, "I want to go to Thailand, but I don't know how to set it up." "No problem," he was told. "I'll give you a contact who can arrange everything." A few weeks later he was in bed with one of those children "there . . . for the picking."

The pedophile made many more trips to Southeast Asia before he was caught. He is currently serving a thirty-year sentence—but he sits in an American prison for having sexually abused American children. He has never been prosecuted for his activities abroad.[4]

• A physics teacher at New York City's prestigious Bronx High School of Science acknowledged during a television interview that he was an active member of NAMBLA. Though the teacher vowed he had never broken the law—and apparently had never been arrested—the school district's subsequent investigation revealed that the teacher had told an undercover investigator he'd had sex with a boy in the Philippines.[5]

• After his release from prison, a convicted child molester enjoyed telling children in his neighborhood that the boys he had "hired" in Thailand charged only eight or nine dollars. He was considering moving there, he added shortly before he disappeared, to take advantage of that country's "more mature cultural attitudes."[6]

The World Discovers a Plague

Though child sex tourism is not new, only in the last few years has it been discussed in the mainstream media. As Chuan Leekpai, Prime Minister of Thailand, told an international conference on the child sex trade in June 1994:

> [T]his problem has not arisen just in the last year or two. It started long ago, but in the past it was not taken as a serious matter. The world didn't pay much attention to it; there was no organization working on this problem; there was no governmental policy, either written or spoken, regarding this problem and there was no international traffic of prostitutes from one country to another. However, all these things have now occurred and Thailand (like other countries in the region) must face the problem.[7]

One of the reasons Thailand was forced to confront this issue was the founding of the organization to which Prime Minister Chuan referred in his address. The organization is ECPAT, an acronym for End Child Prostitution in Asian Tourism. Founded in 1991, within three years ECPAT had established offices and support groups in more than two dozen countries.[8] It has chosen to focus on "four countries in Asia where the situation seem[s] worst—Sri Lanka, the Philippines, Taiwan and Thailand."[9]

Thailand, where ECPAT is headquartered, has drawn the most attention.[10] By all accounts, the rapid growth of that country's tourism and sex industries began in the 1960s.[11] By 1993, one Thai professor was estimating that the sex trade brought in $1.5 billion annually.[12]

The travel industry and the Thai government itself have overtly promoted sex tourism. When the Tourism Authority of Thailand dubbed 1987 "Visit Thailand Year," its slogan was: "The one fruit of Thailand more delicious than durian [a native fruit]—its young women."[13] A travel brochure in England referred to Thais as "Peter Pans—eternal children who have never grown up" and "the most sensual and overtly sexual [people] on earth." Promoting a trip to Pattaya, Thailand's major sex resort, the brochure added:

> If you can suck it, use it, eat it, feel it, taste it, abuse it or see it, then it's available in this resort that truly never sleeps. Pattaya is not for prudes.[14]

Another promotion that was widely publicized appeared in the form of a "postcard" in an Austrian airline's in-flight magazine. This advertisement contained an even more blatant appeal to pedophiles. "From Thailand with Love," read the caption on the front, illustrated by a drawing of a prepubescent girl naked from the waist up. The back of the card, signed by a group of supposed travelers, praised the cornucopia of sexual pleasures they were enjoying around town.

"Got to close now," the card concluded. "The tarts in the Bangkok Baby Club are waiting for us."[15]

One Million Children Prostituted Worldwide

Just how many children are prostituted in Thailand and the rest of Asia? There is no way to know. The prostitution of children is at least nominally illegal in the countries ECPAT monitors,[16] so there can be no official count. However, ECPAT has compiled what it considers to be conservative estimates based on the available information. The numbers are shocking: 60,000 children in the Philippines, 200,000 in Thailand, one million worldwide.[17] But ECPAT doesn't dwell on these figures. It has tried, instead, to reveal the people behind the statistics.

In 1984, five young girls who had been imprisoned in a Thai brothel were burned to death in a fire. Later it was revealed why they'd never had a chance: They had been chained to their beds.[18]

The reality for children in Thai brothels—whether or not they are shackled—is that they are indeed slaves.[19] Many are from small villages far from Bangkok—so many, in fact, that some entire villages are devoid of young girls.[20] Some are kidnapped by pimps or middlemen who sell them. In other cases, parents are tricked by brothel owners, who promise children educational opportunities or attractive jobs in Bangkok. In still other instances, parents sell their children outright or indenture them by accepting "loans" against their children's future earnings (the nature of which the parents may or may not understand). If parents later suspect the worst, they don't have the resources to locate and rescue their distant children.[21]

Once they are warehoused in the brothels, the captured children have this in common: Their lives are completely controlled by their "employers," who often enforce their will with violence.[22]

For this reason, the term *child prostitute* is really a misnomer. These children have been prostituted—and the responsibility lies solely with their exploiters. For adults, prostitution may be a career choice, and some even call it a "victimless crime." But for children in sexual servitude, there is no choice—and *they* are the victims.

Enter the AIDS Epidemic

Aside from the physical and psychological damage these children suffer,[23] they face the increasing likelihood that they will be infected with HIV. "AIDS is now sweeping across Asia at a pace at least as rapid as the virus took in its 1980–85 race across Africa," World Health Organization officials reported in August 1994, at the 10th International Conference on AIDS.[24] Thailand, for obvious reasons, has been particularly hard hit. Estimates vary, but a conservative guess is that at least 500,000 of its citizens were infected with HIV in 1994; by the year 2000, the number will have soared to at least 2.5 million.[25]

Fear of AIDS has proved a windfall for child sex tour operators who, alert to the tourists' anxieties, advertise the youngest children as the safest. They assure nervous customers that the children have regular checkups and that you can't catch AIDS from a child. Neither claim is true.[26]

AIDS and the relentless siphoning of children from the villages have depleted the brothels' supply. This, in turn, has sent brothel owners scouring the region for fresh sources. The result has been trafficking across national borders. Human Rights Watch has exhaustively documented the kidnapping of Burmese women and girls who are deposited in Thai brothels.[27] ECPAT has also noted parallel trails from China and Laos.[28]

Searching for Signs of Progress

Even in the face of this reality, ECPAT points to evidence of progress. Sometimes this progress is measured in small increments: an article here, a conference there, a speech like Prime Minister Chuan's.

Sometimes there are larger signs. Australia, Germany, and the United States have recently passed laws that allow prosecution of child sex tourists upon their return home.[29]

Norway and Sweden already had such laws on the books and have demonstrated a desire to use them.[30]

Still, it is far from certain that these laws will prove effective. A law professor assessed the prospects of Australia's legislation as it neared enactment:

> The enactment of such legislation will be an important symbolic and political statement. However, there is a real danger that, if the legislation is not accompanied by effective enforcement measures at the national and international level, its promises could turn out to be rather hollow. . . . Prosecuting a sexual offence where a child has been the victim is a difficult enough task in any event; when it is further complicated by the problems of obtaining evidence in a foreign country, ensuring the willingness of witnesses to testify in that country where proceedings are conducted in a foreign language, that task becomes even more onerous. Furthermore, the reasons for the lack of effective enforcement of local laws in certain countries may also result in a lack of the close law enforcement cooperation needed to put together a case of this sort.[31]

Some of the staunchest supporters of the Australian law concede that it would be preferable for child sex tourists to be prosecuted in the countries where they commit the crimes.[32] What's more, shortly before these laws were passed, there was optimism that Thailand and its neighbors would strengthen their own laws and—at long last—enforce them. Prime Minister Chuan himself announced in 1992 that he intended to wipe out the child sex trade "in the next two or three months."[33]

Nearly two years later, at an ECPAT conference in Bangkok, the prime minister was forced to acknowledge failure. Once again he declared his hope that he could eradicate the prostitution of Thai children while acknowledging, with surprising candor, what critics had been saying for years: that Thai officials not only condone the practice but, in his words, "[s]ome officials even sponsor this kind of business and share the profits."[34]

Planning for the Future

Despite such setbacks, ECPAT officials appear undaunted. Their plans include expanding the scope of their program to include Africa, Latin America, and other affected regions; providing direct support to local organizations working to heal children who have escaped from prostitution and to safeguard those at risk; convening an international congress in 1996 to seek ways of ending the child sex trade; and developing a comprehensive database that incorporates new research.

In general, ECPAT has chosen to avoid confrontation. It has pursued change by lobbying government officials and by educating the public—largely through the media and through leafleting campaigns arranged with the cooperation of legitimate representatives of the tourism industry. ECPAT has also led a major push to secure U.S. ratification of the United Nations Convention on the Rights of the Child. The United States, which helped draft the document, was one of only fifteen countries (as of August 1994) that had neither signed nor ratified it. Ironically, even Thailand is a party to the Convention.[35]

Critics Tire of Waiting

Not everyone is satisfied with ECPAT's approach—or with the efforts of the U.S. government, which so far have been limited to legislation permitting the prosecution of child sex tourists when they return.

Dorothy Thomas advocates a more aggressive campaign. Thomas is the Human Rights Watch project director who oversaw the investigation of trafficking of Burmese women and children into Thailand. Testifying before a House subcommittee, Thomas was sharply critical of the U.S. State Department's classification of forced prostitution in Thailand as "discrimination" rather than slavery or forced labor. This was, she explained, much more than a semantic quibble. The classification "exempts this abuse from consideration under Section 502 of the Trade Act, which obligates the U.S. Trade Representative to review workers' rights when deciding which countries to designate as U.S. trade beneficiaries." A moment later she continued:

> [T]he State Department has documented the complicity of Thai police and border officials in trafficking of women and girls from neighboring countries into Thailand for forced prostitution since 1991. Meanwhile, the U.S. has [provided] and is continuing to provide police training and [to] sell arms and equipment to the Thai police, including the border police, without ever investigating their involvement in trafficking and forced prostitution.[36]

When there have been police crackdowns, the main target, Thomas said, "has been the trafficking victims themselves."

> In virtually every case that we investigated, the women and girls were apprehended while the brothel owners, pimps, procurers and customers remain free. Moreover, despite clear evidence of official complicity and even direct involvement, we know of no case where a police officer was prosecuted for involvement in trafficking and forced prostitution specifically.[37]

At a minimum, Thomas argued, aid to the Thai police[38] should be contingent on "progress toward prosecuting and convicting culpable members within their ranks. . . . Not only aid," she concluded, "but also U.S. trade relationships with Thailand should be subject to the same vigorous concern for Thai official complicity in the traffic of women and girls."[39]

The Threat of International Pressure

Demands like these have not been lost on Prime Minister Chuan, who by early 1993 had sensed a change in public perception. "Prostitution in Thailand, particularly child prostitution, has reached a state where it is not acceptable to both the country and the international community," he observed. "The prostitution problem also leads to other problems such as international pressure not to buy goods from countries where children are exploited."[40]

A call for the boycott the prime minister so feared was trumpeted a few months later in an American magazine. The final paragraph was a virtual call to arms:

> Thai sex-tourist trade is highly dependent on foreign patrons and vulnerable to an international boycott. . . . A concerted organized and well publicized campaign against child prostitution including a boycott of airlines, travel agencies, hotel chains, and others involved in tourism to Thailand could have a major impact. . . . An international commission of Western notables holding hearings and investigating the violation of the rights of children could provide the necessary publicity to spark the boycott.[41]

For the Children, Nothing Has Changed

To date, however, this declaration of war seems to have had no greater effect[42] than Prime Minister Chuan's pronouncement that he would quickly end the problem. In fact, *no* one's words or actions seem to have had much effect.

The prostitution of children is more widely publicized than ever before, and more people are working to destroy it each year. But for the victims, precious little seems to have changed. And the promised end is nowhere in sight.

David Hechler is an investigative reporter and the author of *The Battle and the Backlash: The Child Sexual Abuse War* (Lexington Books, 1988). He holds master's degrees in teaching (Brown University) and journalism (Columbia University) and is currently a Prudential Fellow for Children and the News at Columbia University's Graduate School of Journalism. He wishes to thank Peggy Healy, R.N., and Lisa Rana, Esq., for assistance in researching this report.

NOTES

1. Not all pedophiles are child molesters. While all are sexually attracted to children, only some choose to act on their impulses. These might be called *predatory pedophiles*. In the interest of brevity, however, in this article they are called simply *pedophiles*.

2. Though NAMBLA is probably the best-known pedophile organization, pedophiles who prefer girls have their own associations and newsletters. *Uncommon Desires*, for example, is a newsletter that describes itself as "the voice of an emerging politically-conscious [sic] girl-love underground."

3. Anon., "Letter to a Young Boy-Lover." *NAMBLA Bulletin* Jan./Feb. 1993, p. 30.

4. Ehrlich, P., "Asia's Shocking Secret." *Reader's Digest* Oct. 1993, pp. 71–72.

5. Gearty, R., "Cortines: Ax Pedophile." (New York) *Daily News* Sept. 22, 1993.

6. Speyer, R., "Freed Molester Pestered Me, Sez Boy." (New York) *Daily News* Aug. 8, 1994.

7. Speech of Prime Minister Chuan Leekpai of Thailand, as reported in: End Child Prostitution: Report of an International Consultation on Child Prostitution Held in Bangkok June 13 and 14, 1994. Published by ECPAT, 1994.

8. End Child Prostitution, p. 9.

9. O'Grady, R., *The Child and the Tourist* (Bangkok: ECPAT, 1992, in association with Auckland, New Zealand: Pace Publishing, 1992), p. 132.

10. Thailand is often used by journalists, sociologists, and political scientists as a case study of sex tourism. As Prime Minister Chuan himself pointed out, the Thai press has a good deal of freedom— as do foreign correspondents working in Thailand. The same cannot be said of all countries in the region. Furthermore, reporters and scholars in Thailand have taken advantage of the opportunity. Their published work, in turn, makes the country that much more attractive to colleagues, who can build on this foundation.

11. See, for example, Sachs, A., "The Last Commodity: Child Prostitution in the Developing World." *World Watch* (July/Aug. 1994): 28. It is important to add that the expansion of the sex trade was due not simply to tourism but to increasing local demand as well. See O'Grady, *Child and Tourist*, pp. 96–97.

12. Ireland, K., "Wish You Weren't Here: The Sexual Exploitation of Children and the Connection with Tourism and International

Travel." Working Paper of Save the Children (London), Sept. 1993, p. 31.

13. Ireland, pp. 45–46.

14. Ireland, p. 51. The brochure was published by Redwing Holidays.

15. O'Grady, R., *The Rape of the Innocent* (Bangkok: ECPAT, 1994, in association with Auckland, New Zealand: Pace Publishing, 1994), p. 54. The airline was Lauda Air, owned by former race-car driver Niki Lauda.

16. O'Grady, *Child and Tourist*, pp. 91–109.

17. This statistic—one million children worldwide—is derived from a 1988 estimate by the Norwegian government. During a 1994 conference, ECPAT presented its own estimate that one million children were prostituted in Asia alone. See End Child Prostitution, p. 10.

18. Ireland, p. 34.

19. O'Grady, *Child and Tourist*, pp. 39–54; and O'Grady, *Rape*, pp. 11–22. *Webster's Third New International Dictionary* defines *slavery*, in part, as "submissiveness to a dominating influence: subservience" and "control by imposed authority: subjection."

20. Ireland, p. 34.

21. The plight of such parents was illustrated by on-camera interviews in the BBC documentary "Dying for Sex" (1993), produced by Giselle Portenier and reported by Peter Godwin.

22. *A Modern Form of Slavery: Trafficking of Burmese Women and Girls into Brothels in Thailand* (New York: Human Rights Watch, 1993). See also note 19.

23. O'Grady, *Child and Tourist*, pp. 115–19.

24. Garrett, L., "Covert Sex Practices Put Asians at Risk." *New York Newsday* Aug. 16, 1994.

25. O'Grady, *Rape*, pp. 78–79. To put these numbers in context, Thailand's population is about 55 million, of whom 6 million live in Bangkok. (Source: *Thailand* [Knopf Guides] [New York: Alfred A. Knopf, 1993], p. 314.)

26. O'Grady, *Rape*, pp. 76–78. See also Garrett, who, referring to reports presented at the 10th International Conference on AIDS, writes: "Fear of AIDS is now driving an active trade in Burmese girls, who are sold by their parents to Thai brothel brokers. Thai men believe these girls—who are usually sold as virgins—are HIV-safe. Of course, these women, according to reports at the conference, eventually catch HIV from their clients and return to Burma, taking the virus with them."

27. *Modern Form of Slavery*.

28. O'Grady, *Rape*, pp. 29–31. ECPAT has also documented trafficking in the reverse direction: Thai children are sold to brothels in Japan, Hong Kong, Taiwan, Australia, and the United States, among other countries.

29. Australia's Crimes (Child Sex Tourism) Amendment Act 1994 became law in July 1994; Germany's amendment to Section 5 of the Penal Code took effect in June 1993; and the U.S. Child Sexual Abuse Prevention Act of 1994 was part of the Crime Bill signed into law in September 1994.

30. O'Grady, *Rape*, pp. 97–99.

31. Byrnes, A., "Extraterritorial Criminal Legislation Against the Sexual Exploitation of Children by Australians Abroad." Paper presented at First World Congress on Family Law and Children's Rights, Sydney, Australia, July 5–9, 1993, pp. 3–4.

32. Bernadette McMenamin, National Coordinator of ECPAT, Australia, testified before the Australian House of Representatives' Standing Committee on Legal and Constitutional Affairs: "Ideally, we would prefer that the offender be punished in the country in which the crime is committed." Transcript of Inquiry into the Crimes (Child Sex Tourism) Amendment Bill 1994, May 1994, p. 4.

33. O'Grady, *Rape*, p. 89.

34. See note 7.

35. The treaty defines the rights of children, including their right to be protected from all forms of abuse. As of August 1994, 166 nations had ratified, nine had signed with the anticipation of ratifying, and fifteen had done neither. The U.S. was the only Western industrialized country in the last group. (Information provided by UNICEF.)

36. Thomas, D., "Sexual Exploitation of Women & Children." Testimony before the House Subcommittee on International Security, International Organizations and Human Rights, March 22, 1994, p. 7.

37. Thomas, p. 3.

38. It is worth noting that in 1994, the U.S. Congress passed The Rhinoceros and Tiger Conservation Act to provide funds that will assist Asian countries' law enforcement efforts to protect these animals from poachers (*Wildlife Conservation* Feb. 1995, p. 7). The countries receive no such funds to assist law enforcement efforts to protect prostituted children. By contrast, Burmese dissident Aung San Suu Kyi herself donated to Thailand $15,000 from her Nobel Peace Prize to assist children in prostitution (O'Grady, *Rape*, p. 89).

39. Thomas, p. 8.

40. O'Grady, *Rape*, p. 90.

41. Petras, J., and T. Wongchaisuwan, "Thailand: Free Markets, AIDS, and Child Prostitution." *Z Magazine* Sept. 1993, p. 38.

42. The absence of any discernible impact may have to do with the small circulation (26,000), and relative obscurity, of the magazine in which it appeared. Then again, there may not be a constituency that approves of these methods.

Myths may expose Evil
But cannot battle it
alone.
Now that you know the Evil
You know what to do.
Now . . .

For more information, and what you can *do* about the situation, contact:

ECPAT (End Child Prostitution in Asian Tourism)
475 Riverside Drive • Room 621
New York NY 10115 USA

Human Rights Watch
485 Fifth Avenue
New York NY 10017 USA

Don't! Buy! Thai!
328 Flatbush Avenue • Suite 311
Brooklyn NY 11238 USA